THE SHAPING VISION OF
GERARD MANLEY HOPKINS

The Shaping Vision of
GERARD MANLEY HOPKINS

ALAN HEUSER

ARCHON BOOKS
1968

To
Archie, Mac, and two Barbaras

CONTENTS

PREFACE

THIS essay is an attempt to trace out in full a theme which links Hopkins' work from first to last: the theme is 'shaping vision'—a vision creative, of creation, in development. The vision is essentially primitive and ultimately mystical, but it receives continual theoretical exegesis by the curious mind of the poet, priest, and scholar Hopkins. Pre-Raphaelitism, Platonism, Scotism, as well as science and three arts (painting, poetry, music), play their parts in working out the vision which inspires so much of Hopkins' writing. A discussion of this theme and of the forces involved should encourage a juster appreciation of Hopkins as artist and thinker.

The book originated from reflexion on the inadequacies of my two longer dissertations, one on poetic imagery, the other on aesthetic cognition, of Hopkins. Among those who helped in the old projects I am indebted to the late Professor Algy S. Noad of McGill University, to Professor Douglas Bush of Harvard University, to the Rev. Daniel N. Dwyer, S.J., of Boston College, as well as to the librarians of McGill University, Harvard University, Boston College, and Boston Public libraries. In 1952 the Rev. D. Anthony Bischoff, S.J., generously supplied me with facsimiles of Hopkins' manuscripts in his possession.

An intramural grant from Princeton University in 1953 allowed me to consult the original manuscripts in England. A similar grant from McGill University in 1955 allowed me to write the first draft of this essay. Among the many who assisted me in England I have to thank Mr. G. W. S. Hopkins, Dr. R. W. Hunt of the Bodleian Library, the late Humphry House, the Rev. Philip Caraman, the Rev. Thomas Corbishley of Campion Hall, as well as librarians of the British Museum and of Pusey House. The Rev. Christopher Devlin, S.J., commented on my doctoral dissertation and kindly loaned me typescripts of his unpublished essays. For later help I

vii

Preface

am indebted to the librarians of Princeton University, the Peabody Institute, Johns Hopkins University, New York Public, and General Theological Seminary libraries. Other debts in correspondence, conversation, and published scholarship would take much space to record. There remains my gratitude to Professor A. E. Malloch of McGill, my friend and colleague, for reading over this study in its latest form, and to the staff of the Oxford University Press for care in seeing the book through the press.

A quick and easy scheme of reference to the works of Hopkins has been used in parentheses in this book. The poems are referred to by number in *Poems of Gerard Manley Hopkins*, ed. W. H. Gardner, 3rd ed. (London, 1948), 5th imp. rev. with additional poems (1956). The prose is referred to by capital Roman numeral (volume) and Arabic numeral (page), according to the following:

I. *The Letters of Gerard Manley Hopkins to Robert Bridges*, ed. Claude Colleer Abbott (London, 1935, 1955);

II. *The Correspondence of Gerard Manley Hopkins and Richard Watson Dixon*, ed. Claude Colleer Abbott (London, 1935, 1955);

III. *Further Letters of Gerard Manley Hopkins including his Correspondence with Coventry Patmore*, ed. Claude Colleer Abbott, 2nd ed. rev. and enlarged (London, 1956);

IV. *The Note-Books and Papers of Gerard Manley Hopkins*, ed. Humphry House (London, 1937).

A. H.

Montreal
March 1958

INTRODUCTION

READERS of Hopkins belong to three groups—those who
accept and seek, those who reject, and those who accept
or reject with qualifications. The disagreement was established
early among the three friends and fellow-poets who corresponded with Hopkins in his maturity: R. W. Dixon, recog-
nizing the importance of what he read, gave unqualified praise;
Coventry Patmore could not penetrate beneath the bewildering surface; and Robert Bridges, often offended at the sub-
stance of the poems which he cherished nevertheless, praised
some things and established dogmas about what he did not
like. Hopkins' readers in the 1870's and 1880's also included
his parents, two sisters, the editor and sub-editor of the *Month*
who rejected both wreck-poems submitted to them, and two
companions in the Society of Jesus (I. 196–7). The three poets
with whom Hopkins exchanged critical letters remained the
important readers; together they made up a Victorian literary
circle mastered by Hopkins' intellect. The unpublished Hopkins
was consulted by his published friends for careful criticism of
their poetry; they urged him in vain to publish. The fame he
recommended to them he rejected for himself, and poetry
played a minor role alongside his religious vocation (I. 231;
II. 88, 148–9). His was the Way of the Cross: he was to succeed
by failure. Not until 1918 were the *Poems* published by
Bridges, then Poet Laureate. The two later editions by Charles
Williams in 1930, by W. H. Gardner in 1948, added further
poems and enabled Hopkins to reach an ever wider public,
from modern poets to common readers. In the 1930's the
demand for more Hopkins material was supplied by Lahey's
brief life and by a good deal of prose—three volumes of letters
edited by C. C. Abbott, and a volume of diaries, journals,
essays, sermons, notes in a model edition by Humphry House.
Today, with the reissue of the prose volumes in expanded
form in 1955–9 and with a prospective life in two volumes,[1]

1

Introduction

Hopkins has come into his own as a Victorian poet fit to take his place beside Tennyson, Browning, Arnold, and perhaps ahead of them in the nineteenth century.[2] His fame is assured. Readers may disagree about interpretation, may need explanation such as this book attempts to supply, but all are aware of the significance, of the permanence of his work.

Hopkins (1844–89), the eldest in an Anglican family of nine children, was raised amid the genteel arts: his father and uncle were small poets; an aunt taught him to sing and to paint. At Highgate School, where he was called 'Skin', he combined writing and sketching activities in Pre-Raphaelite manner, thought of becoming a painter, wrote sensuous verse. He won a poetry prize in 1860 and three years later, in spite of altercations with his obtuse headmaster, he won an exhibition to Balliol College, Oxford. At Oxford Hopkins had some liberal men as teachers and tutors (Jowett, Riddell, Pater, Green), but he was swept into the tractarian movement against liberalism led by Pusey's disciple Liddon. He argued out his thoughts in tutorial essays, turned from sketch-books to journals of descriptive prose, cultivated new modes of verse— metaphysical, epigrammatic, dramatic—and, most important, wrote occasional lyrics reflecting his religious development. By 1865 Hopkins was an ardent Anglo-Catholic of strict devotion, treasuring the poetry of George Herbert and Christina Rossetti, following the ill-starred A.P.C.U.[3] for Anglican-Roman-Orthodox union in the years of Newman's *Apologia* (1864) and Pusey's *Eirenicon* (1865). His conversion, 'all in a minute', came in mid-July 1866; Newman received him into the Roman Church in October, despite the letters that Liddon and his parents sent after him. The zealous convert, called by Jowett 'the star of Balliol', now exhorted by Newman to apply himself to his studies, took a first in the Greats course when he left Oxford in June 1867. He began teaching at Newman's Oratory School. Next spring, resolving to be a priest and religious, he applied to the Society of Jesus. Before a tour of Switzerland in July, he burnt his finished verses

2

Introduction

(what remain are working copies) and afterwards entered the
Jesuit novitiate in September.

Before ordination Hopkins passed through three periods of
intensive training and one of teaching—the novitiate (1868–
70) at Roehampton, the course of philosophy (1870–3) at
Stonyhurst where in mid-1872 he discovered Scotus, a lecture-
ship (1873–4) at Roehampton where he began to develop his
verse theory, and the course of theology (1874–7) at St.
Beuno's College, North Wales, where at last his Muse sang out
after a long self-enforced silence.[4] His triumphal ode, *The
Wreck of the Deutschland*, was followed by exuberant poems,
all employing a new expressional texture, diction, and rhythm
to communicate his vision of creation. He exchanged letters
with a fellow-poet, Bridges. The hidden years came to an end
when he was ordained in September 1877. Between the Welsh
'consolation' and the Irish 'desolation' there intervened the
practical experience of a pastorate among the English—
administrative duties at Chesterfield, preaching in London
and Liverpool, a mission at Oxford where his poetry noticeably revived, and two wearying years in Lancashire in the face
of miserable social conditions. He was diligent in his work,
kept a sermon-book, could afford little time for poetry. A cir-
cumstantial element and priestly concern for souls entered his
verse; sometimes in lesser pieces a forced emotionalism would
result. After the rejection of his wreck-poems by the *Month*,
he sought out another obscure fellow-poet, Dixon, and began
correspondence with him.

For his tertianship (1881–2) he returned to Roehampton;
there he wrote down the fruit of many meditations in a commentary on St. Ignatius' *Spiritual Exercises*, drawn from his
accumulation of Scotist notes. The commentary fell on deaf
ears. The rest of his life was spent in teaching. First he went
to Stonyhurst (1882–4), where he wrote the 'Preface' to his
poems on sprung rhythm and where he struck up a friendship
with the poet Patmore. Finally he was elected Professor of
Greek at University College, Dublin (1884–9). There he
suffered intense spiritual dryness and nervous prostration

3

which wrung from him a group of anguished sonnets. In his last poems Hopkins achieved a more submissive fortitude and faith. These final years were given over to many academic schemes for publication, all of which failed of completion, to musical composition as well as a return to drawing. He died unexpectedly of typhoid fever in June 1889. A brief 'character' of Hopkins—Catholic, English, Oxonian, Tory—must embrace both the speculative Greek scholar of many eccentricities and the dedicated Jesuit priest of honesty and suffering. To the end he remained loyal to his order: 'I have never wavered in my vocation, but I have not lived up to it' (II. 88).

Hopkins' manuscripts originally comprised a very large collection of materials accumulated over thirty years and kept in desk drawers and filing boxes in his room at University College, Dublin.⁵ Upon his death the papers, although willed to the English Jesuits, were sadly dispersed, much inevitably destroyed or lost, including the will itself only lately recovered. One family of manuscripts was acquired by Bridges: poems, letters, sketch-books, musical exercises, spiritual notes. Bridges kept his scrapbook of the poems, the letters to him and to Dixon; eventually he sent the rest off to Hopkins' parents, and in time this material was distributed among their descendants. Hopkins' sisters acting in good faith destroyed a spiritual diary. Recently, after the death of Lionel Hopkins in 1952, most of the Hopkins collection—heretofore kept at Amen House, London—was acquired by the Bodleian Library, Oxford. New family letters were found and added to the Bodleian collection. The Bridges collection—once kept by the Poet Laureate's daughter Mrs. Daryush—is now in the hands of his son Sir Edward Bridges. Another family of manuscripts, what remained in Hopkins' desk and room in Dublin, was scattered mainly among Jesuits in Ireland and England: diaries, journals, essays, sermons, lecture notes, retreat and spiritual notes, a sketch-book, musical compositions, classical notes, annotated books, letters. Much of this material, coming together in 1909 when Father Keating published a memoir, in 1930 when Father Lahey published a life, eventually found

4

its way to Campion Hall, Oxford. But more papers, including a new journal and new poems, have turned up in Jesuit houses. There are manuscripts still uncollected or unaccounted for. It is to be earnestly hoped that some day a ten- or twelve-volume edition of the complete manuscripts will be undertaken.

Hopkins' critics, ever since Bridges, Dixon, and Patmore, have varied greatly in reliability.[6] The principal names may be singled out here. John Pick in a short book, dividing the life into convenient periods and supplying much of the religious context, has provided the best general introduction to his subject. W. H. Gardner, dealing at length with background and poetic influences in a two-volume study, clumsy but always instructive, gives the fullest treatment to date. W. A. M. Peters, S.J., has taken one key, 'inscape' (his definition is open to serious question),[7] and staked out new territory to explore in language. Some American Jesuits under Norman Weyand as general editor have compiled a study which is very disappointing: only a few of the essays are real contributions (Walter Ong on sprung rhythm, the factual articles). Other small studies have been superseded, although the Hopkins issue of *New Verse* (April 1935) and that of *The Kenyon Review* (republished in book form), still contain valuable information with flashes of insight. Two English Jesuits have done some of the best work in the field: Martin D'Arcy, whose few pages on Hopkins' biography and philosophy are very cogent, and Christopher Devlin, who has clarified Hopkins' spirituality along with the Ignatian and particularly the Scotist influences. House and Gardner have been the most reliable editors. These are the chief names. Except for a few valuable discussions, there is a huge backwash of impressionistic, partisan, and misleading writing. In the 1930's and 1940's two schools 'adopted' Hopkins—new critics and poets on the one hand, fellow-religionists on the other. And not a year passes without still another inevitable article on *The Windhover*, perhaps the most discussed poem of modern criticism.

Introduction

The purpose of the study undertaken in these fifteen chapters is to set forth Hopkins' distinctive 'shaping vision', a vision of creation, from its beginnings in Pre-Raphaelite sensationalism and Greek philosophy, through its modifications and applications, psychological, poetic, moral, theological, to its final stages of discovery. Generalizations have been made about Hopkins' vision—usually exclusively Ignatian and Scotist in treatment—but there has been no attempt to trace its full course of development from origins to last speculations, nor any effort made to examine many attendant aesthetic problems.[8] Some of the principal questions can be set forth briefly.

Why does Hopkins' primary vision of creation demand a secondary theory? To what extent do Pre-Raphaelite and Greek ideas influence the theory? How is it applied: (1) to poetic matters, especially to sprung rhythm? (2) to human nature, with the Christian ideal of sacrifice? (3) to the spiritual world, involving the interaction of grace and free will? The theory acquires a new vocabulary: how are the chief idea-words 'inscape', 'instress', and 'pitch' to be understood?

What is the place of the three arts of painting, poetry, and music in Hopkins' development? Why his furious sketching and note-taking? Why his search for colour-chords in paintings? What is behind the sudden outburst of poetry with a new verse theory after a long poetic silence? Why does he as suddenly invade the field of music in later years? What is the nature of his fascination for numbers and ratios? How are the speculative activities of later years to be related to one another?

Finally, how is Hopkins' poetry related to his religion? How do poetic and spiritual matters interact, particularly in the intense experiences of inspiration and desolation? To what purpose does the Christian priest cultivate Greek studies, and what is the use which the Christian poet makes of pagan materials?

These are only some of the leading questions which confront the student of Hopkins' vision. This study merely begins to

6

answer them. For convenience the investigation has been divided into four stages: the early aesthetics of the formative years, a secret build-up of material in the years of training, the outburst and full flowering of maturity, the 'scaffolding' of the last years. Vision and theory are traced in growth and variation. Technical terminology has in general been avoided. Usually the writer has preferred to use Platonic and Augustinian terms in dealing with Hopkins' philosophy of vision— before, during, and after its Scotist phase (1872–84)—rather than confine himself to the more difficult concepts of medieval scholasticism.

PART I. ROOTS 1860–1868

1. SCALES OF LIGHT AND SOUND

HOPKINS' world of sensation, founded on a keen eye and a delicate ear, opened for him the complexities of nature in creative movement. His approach to external nature was from the beginning marked by an artist's pursuit of form and composition. All the senses were brought into operation, but the eye and the ear dominated. Form after form was taken up furiously for study until sketched into definition; then, so defined, it was 'consigned to my treasury of explored beauty' (III. 202). The definition took shape on paper under the guidance of 'a Ruskinese point of view'—that is, a visionary literalism true both to ideal type and to real fact, which produced the 'naturalistic ideal' of Ruskin and the Pre-Raphaelite school of artists. To achieve this exact vision, Ruskin advised the artist-apprentice in his *Elements of Drawing* (1857) to recover 'innocence of eye', to seize the leading lines of organic form, and to follow his laws of art strictly.[1] This Hopkins did, and, by practising Ruskin's science of art, he made an enthusiastic exploration of typical and tonal patterns essentially dynamic in arch and window, cloud and water, leaf and plant.

In early diaries and sketch-books he recorded minute variations in the phenomena of light and sound, especially the radiance of sunlight and the voices of birds. Natural forms, the objects of Hopkins' alerted senses, were in perpetual motion: the sun rising and setting over prospects of changing colour, melodies soaring and sinking in wind and in bird. Between heaven and earth nature was in flux, generating characteristic beauties which he sought to sketch and define before they sank back into their native elements. At the core of nature was death, the mortality of physical beauty. All

Hopkins' early verse was constructed out of the beauties and changes of light and sound, but the light was ever a sunset, the music he heard a dying fall.

To build up a storehouse of practical information for use in painting and poetry, Hopkins depended upon mathematical and musical sciences, as well as upon his own sensitivity to the dynamics of light and sound. In the manner of Plato and the Pre-Socratics, physics and metaphysics were closely joined. The principle of analogy, correspondence, and 'echo' became central in Hopkins' constant paralleling, not only of his three arts—painting, poetry, music—but also of his art-principles as he extended them to philosophy. One such correspondence which he later called 'the common analogy of colour and sound' (III. 324) was vital in his world of sensation. Colours of the spectrum displayed by white light through a prism and tones of the musical octave both constituted measured or graded scales which were said to be satisfactory analogies of each other. The theory had been put forward by Newton and soon became an important artistic device.[2] Furthermore, Hogarth's *Analysis of Beauty* had distinguished prime tints on the surfaces of objects from 'retiring shades' which gradate or go off by degrees, so that there was another scale by which intensity of light and shade corresponded to pitch of sound. There were then two scales established on musical principles —gradations of colour and of shade—so that by Ruskin's time artists were using colour-charts with full reference to the terms of the sister art (and by reverse analogy, a pseudo-science of colour-music was in vogue in the mid-nineteenth century).[3] Light effects and colour harmonies were especially cultivated by the Pre-Raphaelites who were extending the experiments of Constable and Turner into an ever more radiant naturalism. The rainbow appeared frequently in their painting and poetry, and colour-chords selected from the sevenfold scale became their speciality: often a diad or triad out of the favourite red, blue, gold, and white was played upon in gradated hues.[4]

Light, shade, and colour fill Hopkins' early verse. Although the earliest poem, *The Escorial* of 1860, mentions colours

generally in architecture (No. 1, stanzas 6–8), poems of 1862
describe rainbows and rich sunsets with particular exactness.[5]
Il Mystico (Additional No. 1) applies the science of rainbow
and prism to mystical vision: the rainbow is double, air-
blended, rain-born, lit from heaven, 'All a sevenfold-single
gem', with the prime tints or sacred chord of melting hues,
'Sapphire, jacinth, chrysolite'. The rainbow arc links heaven
and earth 'Whence spring the jewell'd harmonies | That
meet in mid-air'. Not the rainbow but a specific sunset chord
of plum-purple is played upon in *A Vision of the Mermaids*
(No. 2). This chord, made up of the crimson-white radiance of
the sky and blue dyes of the sea, fluctuates in colour-scale,
intensity, depth, projection—a maze of interchanging hues
between sky and sea, shaken to the wind as the sun descends.
Hopkins emphasizes inwardness of vision, blood-light throb-
bing within clouds and providing 'Keen glimpses of the inner
firmament'. The deep sources of light are projected outwards
by radiance, so that crimson light through blue air, crimson
reflexions in blue water give specific effects of purple and rose.
Cloud reflexions 'bloom' on the sea and the blossoms toss in the
air. Reflexions on water, sharpened, spiked by motion, collect
into shoals—personified in mermaids who by a little myth
represent the dynamics of the elements. The poem develops
into an allegory which attributes activities of natural phenomena to preternatural forces. Other early pieces with surer
economy carry forward the science of colour: in *Winter with the
Gulf Stream* a molten sunset runs through the final set-picture
(No. 3; original version in III. 437–8); in *Richard* a rainbow
fills its horn to full wheel and the pink-blue chord is noted in
primroses against bluebells (No. 87, fragment iii). Scales of
shade and hue, centering on blue and red keynotes, were
Hopkins' enthusiasm; musical and modulating colours were
carefully recorded in the early diaries and journals. Red light
kindled many of the objects of vision shining through blue
media of air and water; rose, carnation, vermilion found their
complements in tones of the blue-green scale; the delicate com-
plexions of roses, foliage, sea, and sky were traced and retraced

11

with loving regard. Later, on looking back to his artist years, Hopkins wrote: 'I remember that crimson and pure blues seemed to me spiritual and heavenly sights fit to draw tears once' (III. 38). It is clear from such words as 'lustrous gashes, crimson-white' in *A Vision of the Mermaids*, that Hopkins already found wounds and blood in red light. Red was for him to be the colour of grace released at the passion, as blue was to be the colour of nature in its purity.

Piercing and tuning the vision of heaven on earth, of creation's naturalistic ideal, were the songs of nature, not of art: sometimes explicit melody, an antique music 'Withouten instrument' swelling up through 'the sloping scale' to slumber in 'one sweet, deep, heartbroken close' (No. 2); sometimes implicit music, 'an attuning stress' controlling grey-green shade against red colour (No. 87, fragment iv). Natural sounds meant vocal sound to Hopkins, who listening attentively to voices of birds could imitate the characteristics of each—'Five notes or seven, late and few' of the cuckoo (No. 77), the sky-lark's 'silver rivulet' racing from trickle to cataract (Additional No. 1), 'The bats' wings lisping' (No. 21). Rise and fall of liquid song were brought into relation with the source of light: the mermaids burst into plaintive chant when ranged in half-circle facing the sunset (No. 2); the nightingale strains its windpipe to sing of death as crimson dawn broadens into morning (No. 21); 'the circling bird, | Or bat' cries 'a changeless note' in a half-light (No. 16); the lark, who 'Light and darkness from him flings', releases a gush of ecstasy to the sun 'in lone air' and quenches melody at sunset (Additional No. 1). The musical figure of bird in mystical flight and song was common in Hopkins' early verse and was sometimes elaborately developed—as in an Herbertian trope whereby Love is the dominant in the scale of life and provides 'The authentic cadence' for a dedication of powers (No. 16). In later verse Hopkins continually employed the songs and flights of birds, especially the lark in 1876–7: '*Teevo cheevo cheevio chee*' (No. 100), 'His rash-fresh re-winded new-skeined score' (No. 35).

12

Scales of Light and Sound

The sun sank and the sirens wailed to a close, the lark sank to his nest. Textures of light and sound passed into a common void, death in nature. The senses in themselves could not spiritualize themselves, but, giddied 'with blinding daze', were confounded by 'being's dread and vacant maze' (No. 22). Hopkins desired 'that sense beyond', an inspired or infused faith to kindle sensation into spiritual intuition and to renew the face of the earth beneath the Light of Light. Then eternal morning would burst over creation reborn as an earthly paradise, the naturalistic ideal would be supernaturalized by the presence of the Creator himself: 'He fathers-forth whose beauty is past change' (No. 37).

2. THE SENSES

HOPKINS sharpened his senses both by the sketcher's art and by the measuring sciences of mathematics, optics, and music. As a Pre-Raphaelite disciple he wished all in nature and art to be clear, ringing with rare spiritual purity; yet, beyond Pre-Raphaelitism, he was an earnest classical scholar learning to think in terms of Greek theories of perception. In Greek thought generally, sensation was threefold—in the sensed object, an emission of sense qualities or sensibles; in the sensory passage, a medium to carry the sensibles; in the sensing subject, a receiving organ of potential activity. Organs of sense could not come in contact with objects except through media: for Aristotle and his precursors, sight was due to water in the eye, hearing to air in the ear.[1] So for Hopkins objects cast out elements of light and sound through media of air and water to be received by the subject-senses; the more active and spiritual the senses, the brighter and clearer the passage, the higher and stronger the sensibles, then the more divine and intense the sensation.[2] There were impediments to such visionary sensation when the sensibles were dull and weak, the media too full of 'body', the senses thickened. Hopkins became concerned with all functions of sense, later passing on to considerations of mind conscious and unconscious, although his interest was strongly anchored at the elementary level of sensation.

Nature winding through complicated expressions and shapes was scarcely known, a fascinating maze to which Hopkins responded in kind with 'mazèd eyes' (No. 2, l. 33). Awareness of flux urged upon him the necessity of 'holding' an object or scene to be drawn, of 'catching' one static moment of vision. In early verse he took up the position of observer stationed at the mermaid's rock or at the alchemist's window to survey a nature dispersing itself in change. But he was more than observer in his desire to see beyond the maze, to 'pierce the yellow waxen light | With free long looking' (No. 10). Then the spectator's post became that of the 'fixèd eye', absorbed in contemplation, intent on penetrating to meaning and being, and Hopkins exercised Ruskin's faculty of penetrative imagination: 'it is a piercing pholas-like mind's tongue, that works and tastes into the very rock heart'.[3] Impressions rushing in through the senses to the observing subject, 'The unchanging register of change', were 'measured outwards' from that centre (No. 97). It was the 'all-accepting fixèd eye' which allowed him to measure from a reference-point, himself the focus:

> The earth and heaven so little known
> Are measured outwards from my breast. (No. 97)
>
> And I must have the centre in my heart
> To spread the compass on the all-starr'd sky. (No. 91)

All depended upon the observer's position relative to the object, a subject-object relation. The paradox of the rainbow shining in different quarters to people around a waterfall was a 'knot' of many apparent bows to be untied by the principle of the one and the many—one object of sun on water, many objects to many people (No. 81).[4] The observer's position could bend straight lines into the natural beauty of springing curvature:

> Thus, I come underneath this chapel-side,
> So that the mason's levels, courses, all
> The vigorous horizontals, each way fall
> In bows above my head, as falsified
> By visual compulsion, till I hide
> The steep-up roof at last behind the small
> Eclipsing parapet; yet above the wall
> The sumptuous ridge-crest leave to poise and ride. (No. 12)

Stiff architecture through changing perspectives in the subject-object relation was transformed into the vital organic structure of nature.[5] Thus Hopkins explored 'Bye-ways beauty' deliberately in the Oxford scene of variable 'plesaunce' and recorded 'Those charms accepted of my inmost thought'. As an apprentice to art Hopkins was training himself in

15

general composition, in the arrangement and distribution of forms, masses, shades, colours, by virtue of which he entered into the unifying bonds of a picture or prospect. The scene did not remain flat or dead to his eye, but came to life for him in measured movement—that is, distanced, fore-shortened, levelled in stages or masses, projected forward here and there by light intensity, retiring backward by shadow, and delivered through a medium of clarity or of blue opacity.

Not only were objects three-dimensional vessels of the forces of relation, but also the observer's senses and sensorium were receptacles with potential activity aroused in the process of sensation. The observer, the fixed register of sense-impressions, became the focus both of reception, acceptance, and of quickening participation, with reactions of pleasure and pain —pleasure in finding unity of form, pain in feeling the object without unity. Keen senses gave extremes of sweetness and bitterness, delight and torment, which Hopkins applied to the spiritual conditions of his *dramatis personae* of 1864: a deserter from Israel, 'Sicken'd and thicken'd by the glare of sand', is subject to sweet sense-delusions of Egyptian plenty (No. 5); Pilate in hell, in stony exile of raging sun and ice, is afflicted by elements turned monstrous upon contact with his nature and longs to feel extreme sharpness of sensations in penitential self-crucifixion (No. 76); an earthly lover at a known love-signal stands 'Thorn-engaged, impaled and pent' (No. 77, l. 18). All three hover in response between two worlds, flesh and spirit, earth and heaven, Egypt and the wilderness, while over them stands a judgement, the judgement of spirit upon the body of sense.[6] In poems of his Oxford years Hopkins testified to the keen piercing of the senses, even more, however, to that 'penetrative element' of spirit (No. 77, l. 130) necessary to spiritualize sensation, for the senses were in themselves blind and lacking 'that sense beyond', faith (No. 22). The world of sensation had to be revitalized, renewed to God, or else rejected for the world of spirit. In the religious verse of 1865–6 the flush and fever of Hopkins' earlier sensationalism were abruptly checked. He gained a tidy metric and a new restraint, but lost full-bodied, aesthetic richness, which he did not regain in verse until 1876–7. There was a powerful overflow of aesthetic observation into the prose journals. In poems such as *The Queen's Crowning, St. Dorothea, Heaven-Haven*, and *The Habit of Perfection* (Nos. 88, 19, 20, 24), Hopkins was showing a withdrawal of the senses leading to a recovery of their innocence in another field, a cloister of paradise earthly or heavenly. True clearing of the senses was spiritual, spiritual purity and clarity required ascetic discipline or mortification of the senses, and mortification elevated sensational quality to spiritual value. In *The Habit of Perfection* the senses were withdrawn one by one to spiritual things, the door of each sense closed in order to welcome Poverty the bride: this was an emptying of the sense-organs, hollow receptacles to be filled in the spirit through silence, surrender, darkness, fasting.[7]

A new country of unfailing springs opened in sky and garden, with lights and waters wrung clear to the senses. Paradise, the heaven-haven, was an eternal South sending messengers to earth with witness or reward, St. Dorothea's basket or Lord William's crown. Hopkins focused on the margin between earth and heaven, where the faithful wife wavered before her husband's ghost on the threshold of her reward (No. 88) and the wondering lawyer gazed through witness to belief (No. 19). They were poised in attitude between heaven and earth—'which be they? stars or dew?'—even as the consciences of other characters, representing the dynamics of sin and grace, hung poised in Hopkins' Oxford verse. It was the religious conscience of their author who turned from the *via media* of his parents to Anglo-Catholicism and from the Church of England to the Church of Rome.

3. THE IDEA OF BEAUTY

IN the fall of 1864 Hopkins had been introduced to some
people in the Rossetti circle, 'the swells' at Gurney's, and had
great hopes for himself in art (III. 214). In the next years,
under the influence of Pater, one of his tutors, he turned
increasingly to a science of aesthetics, and when he gave up
art—at first painting, then poetry—to elect a religious vocation, he intensified studies in philosophy, especially in Plato
and Aristotle (III. 231). While relinquishing artistic ambitions
for himself, he still hoped by keeping careful prose journals
to record the laws and forms of nature, thereby building up
materials for a philosophy of beauty. In the aesthetic nota-
tions of the journals Hopkins adopted something of Pater's
'clear crystal nature' doubly refined by intellectual analysis
and by emotional sympathy—'a constant clearing of the
organs of observation' and a constant penetration into the
energies of the forms analysed.[1] Pater by his attempt to define
essences of beauty in carefully formulated word-codes also
encouraged Hopkins to search through language for precise
idea-images. And behind Pater there stood the more powerful
Ruskin who demanded that art be firmly based on scientific
principles, the Ruskin who unceasingly set up 'laws' of nature.
At Oxford Hopkins read Ruskin, conversed continually with
Pater, and applied the Platonism of his lecturers and tutors to
art. To communicate his vision of nature in the speculative
atmosphere of Oxford, Hopkins had to reduce it to intelligible
form, to theory. His theory was to be scientific, subjecting
everything to measured order and meaning, as well as dialec-
tic, turning all on a few critical principles derived especially
from the study of Greek. Ruskin's laws, Pater's essences,
Plato's ideas, the Pre-Raphaelite naturalistic ideal and colour-
music, Pythagorean music and mathematics, all these entered
his science.

The basis for Hopkins' early theory of nature and art was

18

the statement, 'Beauty therefore is a relation and the apprehension of it a comparison' (IV. 65–6). The relating process
took place in perspective or space and in explorative activity
or time: the vital relations of parts in a whole were seized as
one thing in space, while experienced as falling into order in
time. There were, then, both the single points at which one
could unify all the details of a scene or object, and the
intervals between those stationary or fixed points:

Beauty lies in the relation of the parts of a sensuous thing to each
other, that is in a certain relation, it being absolute at one point and
comparative in those nearing it or falling from it. Thus in those arts
of which the effect is in time, not space, it is a sequence at certain
intervals—elementarily at least. (IV. xxiii)

Beauty was absolute, fixed, at one point in a series of relations;
this absoluteness held and defined the form as the ideal type,
the type in which the idea of the whole was manifested. While
Hopkins as artist was interested in the relation of parts to the
whole in the beautiful form, as theorist he postulated that
intervals within a sequence of forms could be measured—thus
establishing a scale of fixed points in regular series and giving
a scientific basis to his philosophy of beauty. Once the colour-
sound analogy was extended, or if Ruskin's principle of
musical gradation was applied, then the establishment of
fixed types of beauty in sequence was brought to the convenient pattern of music: all relations of points and distances
were like those of notes and intervals in the various chords and
scales of the archetypal art. Pater was soon to write that 'All
art constantly aspires towards the condition of music',[2] but
it was a principle already present in Pre-Raphaelite art and in
Ruskin's art-criticism, a Platonic and Pythagorean concept
now entering Hopkins' theory.

Pater's view of art as deliberate craftsmanship working
according to musical principles was embodied by Hopkins in
his Platonic dialogue *On the Origin of Beauty* (1865), yet with
a scientific turn. He dramatized the unscientific attitude in a
lay student Hanbury, whom he did not spare in exposing,
while the Professor of Aesthetics at Oxford, a Socratic figure,[3]

and the Pre-Raphaelite Middleton were closer to his own point of view. In the course of informal dialogue Hanbury has to admit that beauty depends on objective relations, not merely on subjective responses;[4] that one way of comparing the relations in beauty—one and many, likeness and difference, proportion and parallelism—is by continuous and non-continuous lines, colours, shades, or sounds; and it is decided from the correspondence in gradation between light and sound that there are two kinds of beauty: transitional, with intervals or half-notes, and abrupt, without intervals, or, by application of musical terms, *chromatic* beauty of tonal expression and *diatonic* beauty of structure (IV. 77–8, 84, 93).[5]

Beauty, discovered in the concrete world, referred to an ideal order beyond:

> Beauty it may be is the meet of lines,
> Or careful-spacèd sequences of sound,
> These rather are the arc where beauty shines,
> The temper'd soil where only her flower is found. (No. 91)

Beauty in sky and earth was but a reflexion, a Platonic 'shadow' of real beauty. Hopkins was led from observed forms to their origins in ideas, from the arc of particular beauties to the centre from which the Idea of Beauty shone. And if the fixed types in outward nature were scaled and strung musically, so were their essential ideas in the underlying world of forms. Hopkins passed from art through science to metaphysics. His concept of beauty pointed the way: the subordination of parts in a natural whole was a concrete example of the many particulars and the one universal in an idea. The definition of specific types of beauty in a scale of flux was the way to reach their eternal ideas. As his aesthetics was musical in basis, so was his metaphysics. He had already taken natural songs to represent the spiritual life in his poetry; now into his philosophy entered the singing music of the spirit. Music like architecture provided a useful scientific ground for aesthetics. While science could not be as exactly applied to painting and poetry, yet Hopkins felt the need of science: 'some scientific basis of aesthetical criticism is absolutely needed'.[6] Music and

20

architecture provided this scientific basis in proportion, relations which could be numbered and measured.

Before he left Oxford, Hopkins set forth in Platonist fashion a new Realism to combat the current materialism, a philosophy of flux, 'of a continuity without fixed points, . . . of development in one chain of necessity, of species having no absolute types and only accidentally fixed'. Against all this Hopkins wrote in an important essay, *The Probable Future of Metaphysics* (1867):

To the prevalent philosophy and science, nature is a string the differences in which are really chromatic but certain places in it have become accidentally fixed and the series of fixed points becomes an arbitrary scale. The new Realism will maintain that in musical strings the roots of chords . . . are mathematically fixed and give a standard by which to fix all the notes of the appropriate scale: . . . so also there are certain forms which have a great hold on the mind and are always reappearing and seem imperishable . . . and these things are inexplicable on the theory of pure chromatism or continuity—the forms have . . . absolute existence. It may be maintainable that species are fixed and to be fixed only at definite distances in the string. . . . To ascertain these distances and to point out how they are to be mathematically or *quasi*-mathematically expressed will be one work of this metaphysic.[7]

In addition to fixed forms there were two other articles in the new Realism: against history of growth from parts to the whole, 'Realism will . . . maintain that the Idea is only given . . . from the whole downwards to the parts'; against the modern atomism of personality, Realism will counter 'with some shape of the Platonic Ideas'. Thus Hopkins traced three points, in a preliminary sketch of a metaphysics: (1) fixed types in the string or scale of nature rather than fluctual accidentals; (2) unitive wholes prior to their parts; (3) objective ideas outside of subjective personality. By applying these three points together to his philosophy of beauty, Hopkins arrived at a Platonic theory for the Pre-Raphaelite naturalistic ideal: every fixed form in nature pointed to an underworld of ideal reality, in which its type was established in fullest organization or highest development as one whole, fixed,

21

essential idea. Unity of idea led Hopkins to see in the history of art the rise and fall of types of perfection, and to require in the philosophy of art the identification of those types in terms of truth and beauty. This was Pater's task too. Hopkins was, however, more concerned with the concrete sign in nature. By careful restatement of his Platonic theory of the naturalistic ideal, he was, within a year, to be led to the discovery and formulation of 'inscape'.

4. TWO WORDS OF BEING

How did Hopkins arrive at the puzzling coinages 'inscape' and 'instress'? Were they arbitrary, or did they have a natural growth recoverable to readers? There are three strands in the development—the aesthetic recording of types in nature, the philosophical theory of ideas, the linguistic sharpening of word-codes and idea-images. It may be useful to recall first that in sharpening language to be the living vehicle of thought, Hopkins preferred the spoken word, immediately fresh, and that he gathered quaint words for mimetic and active qualities. In 1864 he had established a theory of the three languages of poetry—Delphic, mere verse, the *genus* poetry; Parnassian, the poet's idiom, the *species* poetry; and inspiration, an abnormal acuteness far beyond both (III. 216–20). In gleaning words for his own use Hopkins was looking for striking, distinctive words, as ringing and immediate to the senses as to the mind. His early diaries contain notes on such words as *horn, fash, grind, crook*, worked out in extensive series of onomatopoetic associations from Saxon, Latin, and Greek roots: for example, '*Grind, gride, gird, grit, groat, grate, greet, krouein, crush, crash, krotein etc.* | . . . Cf. *Crack, creak, croak, crake, graculus, crackle*' (IV. 6). One begins to hear Hopkins' later vowel-music and consonant-chime in these series. The early journals too are full of packed word-codes, often monosyllables. It may be expected that 'scape' and 'stress' were words with well-defined positions in sequences of association and connotation, that 'inscape' and 'instress' were coined from them.

While teaching at Newman's Oratory in 1867–8, Hopkins wrote a careful passage on words, dated 9 February 1868, in a book on the Pre-Socratics entitled *Notes on Greek Philosophy*. Here he identified three terms or moments of a word: (1) power of connotation, called 'prepossession of feeling'; (2) definition, vocal or mental utterance; (3) application, extension to the concrete thing or things designated (IV. 95). The second term was the word proper, not merely in speech, but in thought, 'expression, *uttering* of the idea in the mind.' While the other two terms were not the word proper, the first gave the word its soul and referred to passion, enthusiasm, awakened by the word in 'its evolution in the man and secondly in man historically'. Clearly then, any dialect or coined word much used by Hopkins had a central definition as well as an etymological and individual bias or 'prepossession' full of connotative value. To understand the sometimes bewildering applications of the words 'inscape' and 'instress' it is necessary not only to approach some definition, but even more to discover the 'prepossession' which interconnects and directs them.

'Inscape' and 'instress' were first used by Hopkins in a passage headed *Parmenides*, appearing shortly after the passage on words in *Notes on Greek Philosophy*. Particular Greek texts were preoccupying Hopkins, holding him to the roots of language, at the same time that Plato and the Eleatic School were reminding him of the prior unitive wholeness of ideas. His note on Parmenides, 'the father of Realism', brought the new words 'inscape' and 'instress' into close connexion with the great text *Being is* or *It is*, simple assertion.[1] Being is the One, the Idea of ideas, 'unextended, foredrawn'—that is, traced out beforehand, prior to (in time or position)—what holds everything together, the divine cement, the ligature of grammar and logic *is*, the copula of affirmation *yes*:

> But indeed I have often felt when I have been in this mood and felt the depth of an instress or how fast the inscape holds a thing that nothing is so pregnant and straightforward to the truth as simple *yes* and *is*. 'Thou couldst never either know or say | what was not, there would be no coming at it.' There would be no bridge, no stem of stress between us and things to bear us out and carry the mind over. (IV. 98)

According to this key statement, instress 'feels deep' and inscape 'holds fast' in being. Each has an interior oneness ('in-') which is distinctive: instress gropes downward to unity of being in feeling, while inscape upholds unity of being in

24

fixed position, in fixed shape. Both concepts taken together are closely connected to the 'bridge' or 'stem of stress' which, as the 'prepossession of feeling' in Hopkins' double definition, must not be neglected.

Inscape has been variously defined, most frequently as (1) internal form, 'inshape', soul, idea; (2) ideal structure, excellence of form moulded from within, beauty; (3) natural pattern, unitive glimpse of natural scenery as design of the whole.[2] It is agreed that inscape indicates form of some kind, internal, ideal, natural. The above main classes of meaning are helpful generally, but are not specific enough to cover both Hopkins' connotative uses of the word and its applications. The prepossession of inscape by 'bridge' or 'stem of stress' leads one directly to *scape* (Latin *scapus*, Greek *skapos*) as 'shaft of a column/tongue of a balance/flower-stalk, stem'; while the universal extensions of inscape to cover forms anywhere and everywhere indicate in the background the inclusive word *shape* (Old English ȝesceap with a variant form *scape*) as 'creation, creature/make, structure/decree, destiny'.[3] It is not unlikely that Hopkins' double word meant 'created form held fast by evidence of creative power' (by shaft, tongue, stalk, stem of stress), or, in terms of his Platonic Realism, 'the concrete emblem of a fixed type in the scale of nature, bearing within a sign of the Creator' (a string of creation; later, in the 1880's, a thread of destiny). The origin of the word in the context of a note on a Greek text and its application especially to natural forms of creation tend to support the view represented here. For confirmation, the prepossession can be traced back through Hopkins' earlier vision.

In searching out the fluctual, labyrinthine, three-dimensional complexities of external nature, Hopkins had been concerned with seizing the leading lines of form and with fitting relations among masses flush in composition. Unity, ideality, was to be found in the interior laws of curvature; fullness, reality, in the outer bounds and shapes of curved wholes.[4] At the same time that Hopkins was groping for individual, acute words to identify each specific shape, he was continually defining and redefining in diaries and journals of 1863–8 every shape as a form of unitive curve. This was the eternal preoccupation of the artist, familiar in Hogarth's famous 'serpentine line'—figured inside a solid pyramid on the title-page of *The Analysis of Beauty*—but it had been given new weight by the dynamics of stress in the Romantic school, by the ideality of beauty in the Pre-Raphaelite school.[5] Some particular lines and curves had unusual significance for Hopkins as visible signs of unitive vitality, of creation. His diaries and journals are prepossessed to record (1) rays and beams of light (arc of rainbow, halo, spokes and wheels of light); (2) shafts and stems of wood and stone (plant, tree, pillar); (3) waves and ribs of air and water (current or tide visible in cloud, river, sea, snow).[6] Most of these curves radiated from a single point or around a few points—the root, spring, or focus of their life—which made them wholes of organic shaping. Drawing and sketching the unitive life of objects led Hopkins to participate in the dimensions, relations, and positions of parts in a whole —perspective activated—the whole shape of creation in little or one type of it in detail in a creature. Again, he sketched not one individual form, but the type. This type was fixed or fastened by a string of being, shaft, tongue, stalk, stem; when discovered, the stem-shape gave the key which united and 'locked in' the existential wholeness of a form. It appears, then, that inscape as organic form or naturalistic ideal was a fixed type in the scale of flux, a created structure 'ideal' in living oneness and 'real' in concrete wholeness, held fast to a focus or guiding curve, 'the meet of lines' or the strings of being. The natural form was linked to its essential idea through the fixed type, inscape.

Instress has been more readily defined than inscape. In the *Origin of Beauty* beauty is a relation, the apprehension of it a comparison. In *Parmenides* the energy of the relation or feeling of the comparison is instress in the object, stem of stress between object and subject (mind)—ligature of being in the line pointing to unity within the object, copula of being in an imagined equal sign standing between object and subject.

There are eventually three terms of stress and instress: (1) in the object, depth of feeling as spring of its unity; (2) between object and subject, identity of being through a flash of intuition; (3) in the subject, depth of feeling in response to the intuition of being.

Stress (Old French *estrece*), the equivalent of the Greek *energeia* and the medieval Latin *actus*, means 'force, pressure/strain/emphasis/affliction, straits'.[7] Stress exerts pressure, leaps into lines, strains into life, and so informs the shapes of creatures. It shows itself by twists flung through or out of the forms it inhabits, by rises and falls of feeling in visible and in oral shapes, and by melodic lines of natural songs. Curvature winding through creation, the evidence of life, has the impulse of life behind it. Stress becomes instress when it is linked inwards to depth, origin, and when it gathers to an intensification or response. In instress the feeling in object or subject is drawn to an interior oneness, energy collected to a simple moment of emotion (fervour) or of will (choice).

Now inscape is the one-shape or stem-form, instress the shaping force or stemmed feeling, within creatures of nature and art. Both point to unity of being in a prior idea ('foredrawn') which is the spring of creative life and creative design. The ligature of being and the copula of knowledge are ultimately identical: 'To be and to know or Being and thought are the same' (IV. 100). The bond of feeling is rooted in the same ultimate identity. Therefore, the known shape of a creature, inscape, and its felt life, instress, are linked together to a common 'inbeing' or idea. By virtue of *skapos*/stem, inscape is upheld by instress. By virtue of *ʒesceap*/creation, both inscape and instress have a common root. The pair makes up, then, two words of being. The first word is cognitive form; the second, felt pressure—the knowing and the feeling linked to being through shape and shaping.[8] There is another way of looking at the two words. For inscape is a fixed note in the diatonic scale, abrupt, shaped as one, a type, while instress is a transitional note in the chromatic scale, gradual, sliding between, a motion: the two scales are measured on one string, the string of being. By 1868, then, and before he entered the Jesuit novitiate, Hopkins had arrived at a useful theory for his vision of creation, based on carefully coined words and on prolonged meditation on key texts of classical philosophy. The aesthetic vision reached for metaphysical ground, and natural sensation was thereby ready to receive supernaturalization.

PART II. STORE 1868–1875

5. PSYCHOLOGY OF INSTRESS

HOPKINS' poetic silence during his training in the Society of
Jesus from 1868 to 1875, was part of the hidden life of prayer,
sacrament, and study which stored up within him resources for
a priestly and religious vocation. His main concern was
spiritual growth through the Ignatian discipline, founded on
the *Spiritual Exercises* and the *Institute*. Although no spiritual
diary appears to have survived (there are only later retreat
notes), the large journal of 1868–75 includes some notes of
private character, along with many painstaking analyses and
descriptions of the conduct of external nature. The latter show
how sensation, through new experiences of inscape and instress, was being spiritualized. Periodic mortification of the
senses—such as withdrawal of the eye for a half-year penance
in 1869 (IV. 121)—together with practice of daily meditation,
self-examination, communion, inevitably led Hopkins to a
fuller awareness of God without and of spiritual acts and states
within. He acquired a psychological interest in consolations
and desolations, on levels of mind and soul below consciousness; many of these spiritual affections and psychic feelings
can be understood by reference to St. Ignatius' Rules for the
Discernment of Spirits.[1]

Some depth of sorrow, Christ's agony in the garden, or some
height of joy, procession of the Blessed Sacrament, could at a
single moment of truth be so brought home to him that he
would suddenly weep, without knowing why, without any
apparent reason or explanation. Why? he asked himself. Because great pathos penetrated the soul as a knife into the body,
until striking sideways some force already gathered there it
discharged tears. No 'hit' was possible without personal

reception; yet that reception was entirely unconscious and 'cleared the understanding in its passage': the reason was not aware of it (IV. 128). Spiritual activity below the level of rational thought meant, therefore, that *Pneuma*, the Spirit of God, was acting upon *psyche*, the soul in a man gathered to a oneness below consciousness. The gathering of subterranean feeling was a knot of energy, a potential instress, which could be released in the soul by the activity of an incoming stress from God.

Psychic instress had its opposite in collapse known as 'slack', the suspension of instress. Hopkins noted, in a nightmare when the sense of God sustaining the soul was absent, how the body lost all muscular stress, fell back by force of gravitation upon the soul, hung on the chest ('the seat of *thymos*', spirit, breath) like a dead weight, and crushed out breath.[2] The soul was reduced to feeble whispering; but by using residual sighs to call upon the holy name the soul could gradually regain courage and self-possession (IV. 184–5). Thus, in explaining psychic experiences, Hopkins drew upon his ideas of stress and instress, spiritualized them, and added the reverse term 'slack', so that he had a ready theory for acts in the *psyche*: sudden force, tension, on the fibres of being gave instress; suspension, relaxation, gave slack or collapse.

Such psychic records help a great deal to elucidate the full meaning of instress. Instress was feeling stored in the unconscious, in the well of memory below understanding, in the depths of being, and drawn to a critical moment—either an uncontrolled emotional release or a voluntary choice controlled by reason, depending upon the level on which it acted. The borderline between conscious and unconscious, the level of irrational feeling fascinated Hopkins. He found that unconscious association through feeling could bring about mysterious relations between separate instresses: an instress received externally could provoke a similar one from within. Strong energy (pressure of size in clouds or force of running in roads) provided feeling which linked remembered instresses associated with the same sense (IV. 150, 153–4). Strong impression on the sense of sight could somehow by mysterious feeling ('unconscious cerebration') call up a different sense (humming a tune or tasting brass) with which it was linked crosswise (IV. 127, 179). Feelings were continually falling back to their foredrawn or prior condition of being, and to that extent were independent of time and sense, of immediate stress and scape. Feeling could bridge considerable gaps. The conscious mind was often surprised at the unconscious links.

Inscape too was submitted to psychic pressures. Not only feelings but impressions—images in the mind, later called scapes or species—tended to be absorbed into the memory, there to prepossess or predispose the mind by occasional unconscious influence. Dreaming was a phenomenon of the unconscious in which the senses yet appeared active in some way. Hopkins explained dream images as dead impressions which were suddenly, by a reverse action of the visual nerves, 'lodged' upon the dark field of the eyelid, and 'stalled'— brought into definite position—by the mind (IV. 126–7). This example of subjective inscape thrown up by inner energy proves at the same time that inscape is fixed, for 'lodge' and 'stall' both mean 'to hold or house in a fixed place'. Words like 'lodge' and 'stall', chosen to communicate Hopkins' vision, were characteristic of the journals. One such important word of instress was 'throng' (associated with the German *Drang*), expressing the force of a crowd of stresses.

For Hopkins sensations flowed between stress and slack in the direction of feeling; feelings themselves thronged into stresses, contacted different instresses by association, worked below consciousness; tension or relaxation on the strings of being gave instress or slack. Hopkins' reading of the Franciscan philosopher Duns Scotus, chiefly from 1872 to 1884, was to confirm his own experience, that sensation was a spiritual sense, linked to innate memory, rising out of and falling back to unity of feeling—a breaking from the unconscious to consciousness of the deep realities of stored being.

31

Scotus treated the traditional faculties of the soul (memory, understanding, will) as levels of consciousness, and he encouraged Hopkins to put trust in the primitive levels of feeling, sensation, innate memory, unconscious knowing.

6. INSCAPE

THE inner life of prayer, word, and sacrament heightened Hopkins' vision of the outer world, still seen in precise perspective and glow, but now trembling in cumulative witness to creative power within.[1] What might be called 'divine' geometry and mechanics—for nature contained what was beyond science—went hand in hand with his search through language for the chiselled word-sound. A creaturely shape became a solid 'burl' or 'bole' of many aspects: on the surface, grooves ('cross-hatching') or overlay ('frets' and 'lace'); in section, planar turns ('wards'), corner-angles ('quains'), and declivities along the grain ('cleaves'); in the interior, under-scaping supporting the whole ('ribs' or 'frame'). The journals were packed with solid geometry. The word itself was becoming a fixed type, inscape, a sharp monosyllable or one-shape, rendering immediate sound-sight-touch sensation from living speech—often through dialect survivals of primitive forms. Words were selected to hold fast in shaped sound an inner life, containing the three moments of prepossession, definition, extension. For example, 'cleave' is defined as 'cliff/cleft', but a long vowel boxed in a strong casing of consonants evokes verbal action 'hewn/split', and thus is marked by prepossession 'cleavage' and by extension to fissured rocks or split wood. 'Quain', the sharpened dialect form of 'quoin' or 'coign', which was derived from architecture—a wedge-shaped stone in arch or corner—Hopkins used to stand for radiant planar angles made by star, crystal, and cloud; for the distinctive angle in prismatic section Hopkins chose the dialect form 'quain', itself distinctive, associated with the stellar 'wain' and with the curiously refined 'quaint'.[2]

The individual prospect or object was best seen when 'clear'. 'Clear' did not merely mean the painter's glassy effect, nor only physical bloom, brilliancy, and projection, but the religious' divine penetration by which creatures glowed and

33

radiated from within: 'winged silver slips of young brake . . .
gloried from within'; 'Water . . . lit from within looking like
pale gold' (IV. 175, 177). Heavenly light, *lumen*, gave resplen-
dent clarity to the integrity and harmony of form. So activated, the form could, by application of Platonic 'shadow',
beget a mirror image of itself: one planet reflecting another in
opposite 'bays' of sky, a halo 'rhyming' the moon, a brilliant
fall of leaves standing for the 'cast self' of a tree (IV. 125, 158,
186). Radiance, reflexion, refraction—phenomena noted from
the earliest years—continued to fascinate Hopkins in rainbow
and colour-scales, in ray-spokes and prismatic clouds.

When the wheels of divine geometry spun into action,
geometrical nature became mechanical. Yet even the complex
mechanics of water illustrated origins: in freezing, water on a
potsherd formed an icicle 'like a forepitch of the shape . . . it
grew on', for the shaping idea pre-established the degree of
turning in icicle faces; in evaporating, steam rose by *'aestus*,
throes' of film, timed according to interior moments when
stress of heat overcame surface tension (IV. 136, 139). The sea
too displayed origins, rose in breakers shaped to the coast,
broke in a sequence of swimming scapes, and fell back to a
oneness, 'warped to the round of the world like a coat upon
a ball' (IV. 163, 164, 167). Unity of being in station and in
action controlled creation.

The complexity of unfolding activity, so hard 'to unpack
. . . and law out' in break and flooding of wave, was easier to
'hold' in the gradual process of organic growth and decay.
Here the key word was 'pitch', noted in the degree of toss in
bud and spray of trees (IV. 133, 141) and denoting degree of
acuteness or refinement, point of elevation in the tonal scale,
which determined height of development or organization.[3] In
organic form there was a series of aspects, 'successive sidings'
or modifications of one inscape, discovered in the flag flower's
coming to the pitch of full blowing, in the horned violet's
withering to the slack of decay (IV. 148–9). A whole sequence
running through such changes was a 'behaviour' (IV. 142,
148), while any one attitude was eloquent enough to enter into

speaking relations with the onlooker—the 'bidding' of blue-bells, the folk word for posture of the heads (IV. 174). As inorganic shapes had three- and two-dimensional aspects, so the organic had 'successive sidings' or levels of actualization of ideal form from one pitch to another. The eye was attached by stem of stress to the object, and could 'grow' through levels of development—that is, could feel deeper and deeper instress, or sense higher and higher inscape. The 'mazèd eye', which had become 'fixèd', now became the 'growing eye'. Aristotle's theory of sensation—the participation of object and subject through a medium—became growth in stress and in pitch. Unity of inscape could be achieved by 'stalling' (fixing in position) one part of a scene with another—inscaping sun and sunset together, for example (IV. 129). Where no unity was found, there was no inscape, only a random scaping called 'idiom', a graphic writing peculiar in some way without unify-ing law (IV. 128–9). Where unity was, there were levels of depth and height to be sensed by inscape and instress: for example, the eye in gazing at the intense blue of bluebells could abstract a glare of light 'to float their deeper instress in upon the mind' (IV. 174).[4]

Nature or creation, a system of scales on strings, had many pitched levels reaching down to creative power. Each level had its spiritual intuition. The conversion of sensation to the uses of the spirit was encouraged in St. Ignatius' *Spiritual Exercises*, a book filled with imagery for purposes of prayer, with much advice about 'the application of the senses' in meditation. But why did Hopkins show such extraordinary and characteristic regret at the felling of a tree?

The ash tree growing in the corner of the garden was felled. It was lopped first: I heard the sound and looking out and seeing it maimed[,] there came at that moment a great pang and I wished to die and not see the inscapes of the world destroyed any more[.] (IV. 174)

It was not a mere tree that was felled; it was a creature, an emblem of stemmed oneness testifying to the unity of being between Creator and creation; its key lay in the interior law

35

of stem-shape, power rendered visible. The world of nature was made up of varieties and degrees of such signs—the wave-like stem in leaf and cloud, the 'set' or stem of river current which moulded peat or grass into the clustered shat the curling whip in flame, the home-coiling wire in bushes of spray, and, as above, the holding swerve in timber (IV. 130, 140, 149, 154, 159, 169, 190). These were the laws of inscape displaying the very lines of creation and creative will. They not only guided all nature, but also pointed to the steering Idea or Word of one Being and were, therefore, witness to the Providence of God. Increasingly Hopkins was drawn to acknowledge shapes of natural force as vessels of God's finger—the Holy Ghost sustaining the universe. No longer a little myth of preternatural forces in natural dynamics, mermaids playing in sunset reflexions, but a reality of the supernatural, ultimately Godhead itself. In 1868 when Hopkins looked at precise planing in rocks, 'Nature became Nemesis' (IV. 105): in 1873 when he discovered a springing law of unity even in random clods of snow, he had to admit that 'chance left free to act falls into an order as well as purpose' (IV. 173). However, the keenest evidence was in the night sky and its omens—a comet hanging like a shuttle-cock threatening to fall (IV. 198), Northern Lights 'thrown out from the earthline . . . not following the warp of the sphere':

This busy working of nature wholly independent of the earth and seeming to go on in a strain of time not reckoned by our reckoning of days and years but simpler and as if correcting the preoccupation of the world by being preoccupied with and appealing to and dated to the day of judgment was like a new witness to God and filled me with delightful fear[.] (IV. 135)

It is to be noted that comets and Northern Lights are stringed, that strings or veins convey the force of being. So, when Hopkins felt unwell and downcast, he was reduced to mere existence: 'nature in all her parcels and faculties gaped and fell apart, *fatiscebat*, like a clod cleaving and holding only by strings of root' (IV. 182).

Hopkins did see more than unity of creative source in the

lines of creatures, more than judgement; he saw by unity of redemptive destiny that all creatures were completed in the ideal human nature of the Incarnate Lord. He had this Franciscan insight in the 1860's before he read Scotus.[5] The reading of nature as a series of ideas in the Word of God was most practised in Christian exemplarism, a Platonic tradition handed down from the Greek Fathers through St. Augustine to the Franciscans, such as St. Bonaventure and Duns Scotus.[6] It was through Scotus that Hopkins found his vision of creation capable of metaphysical as well as christological treatment. He first read Scotus' *Opus Oxoniense* in 1872:

> At this time I had first begun to get hold of the copy of Scotus on the Sentences in the Baddley library and was flush with a new stroke of enthusiasm. It may come to nothing or it may be a mercy from God. But just then when I took in any inscape of the sky or sea I thought of Scotus. (IV. 161)

The reading of Scotus confirmed his intuitions (vision) and speculations (theory) about inscape and instress.[7]

For Scotus, nature was a living whole, apart from the individuals or selves possessing it; nature was a real entity because it originated as an idea or type in God's mind prior to his will giving it individuating existence.[8] Individuals were so many degrees in the common nature. All degrees in the common nature were summed up in Christ as Man, who personified nature. If one could have insight, intuition, past the existent creature into its essential nature or idea, one would see the created nature of Christ, for all nature reached out for completion in his ideal Person. Hopkins discovered that Scotus did allow for such an intuition—not through distinct, abstractive understanding, but through unconscious knowing. Unconscious knowing evolved from vague awareness (of nature's created being) to visionary sensation (of nature being created, nature in search of or on the verge of a self, called the *species specialissima*). Below the level of abstraction it was possible to have the sensation of common nature drawn to its innate type, the created nature of Christ. Only when the existent creature was experienced as one with its essential nature (the

37

idea created in God's mind, the underlying type), only then
did the resulting experience equal the *species specialissima.*
Here Hopkins came upon the Scotist equivalent for inscape—
the fixed type between natural form and essential idea.
(Henceforth the one-shape of the creature allowed for vision
of Christ, and inscape could become incarnation.) Furthermore, the creative strain of identifying the existent creature
with its essential idea was stress or instress—stress of God's
activity giving existence to the idea, instress of man's reception, acknowledging and co-operating with the idea behind the
existent. (Henceforth the stemmed pressure of feeling could be
associated with grace in God's act, will in man's response—
stress on God's side, instress on man's.) Hopkins had seen ideal
human features in creation long before he read Scotus. Now
that his insight was validated by the Franciscan philosopher,
he found Christ's created nature as Pattern or Archetype
behind creation—specifically, a sacramental Presence as light
(Christ as *lumen de lumine*); as twofold variegation (the two
natures, human and divine, of Christ); as grain and mould,
seed and wheat (Christ in the eucharist); as angelic spirit
(*anima Christi*)—wherever analogical attributes of Christ
flashed forth in creation.

Before as well as after Hopkins' encounter with Scotus, he
found partially human expressions in shapes of external
nature, seeming to indicate a reaching out for archetypal
Manhood: eyelid in clouds, eyelash in ashsprays, lip in flowers,
shoulder in mountains, limb and foot in glaciers, beard in
waterfalls, taperlit face in snowdrifts. Lower nature aspired to
ideal human nature. Sometimes Hopkins felt called to give
such a general aspiration to Christ: 'As we drove home the
stars came out thick: I leant back to look at them and my
heart opening more than usual praised our Lord to and in
whom all that beauty comes home' (IV. 205). At other times
he was recalled, through inscapes of mixed strength and
sweetness, to a specific intuition of the incarnation: 'I do not
think I have ever seen anything more beautiful than the bluebell I have been looking at. I know the beauty of our Lord by

it' (IV. 133–4). What was the mystery of the bluebell? Was it, because of bent heads, an emblem of obedience or sacrifice? Or was it the perfect beauty blending *claritas* into *integritas* and *consonantia*? It baffled all senses, especially the eye, and gave off unusual light. Probably the bluebell was a sort of altar light standing for the Real Presence, for Christ of the holy tabernacle. Its light shining through Mary's colour of glass-blue represented Jesus incarnate living in Mary,[9] the Light of Light dwelling within immaculate or ideal nature. What the eye did when it abstracted a glare of light from blue-bells 'to float their deeper instress in upon the mind' (IV. 174) was to recognize the Presence of Christ. That deeper instress was a moment of spiritual feeling, acknowledging our Lord indwelling in the pure creation of his original will, even as in the instituted sacrament of his redemptive purpose.

7. ELEMENTS OF VERSE

WHILE the stored resources of aesthetic and spiritual experience had to await an opportunity for expression in poetry, verse theory prepared the way. In 1873–4 Hopkins taught as Professor of Rhetoric at Roehampton and wrote lectures of which some notes remain. At that time he was advancing through Greek, Latin, and English verse models to sprung rhythm. The two lectures available—*Rhythm . . . and verse*, *Poetry and Verse*—show that rhythm was but a part of his total theory which also included vowel-chime and musical notation. The elements cover (1) rhythm (stress), (2) lettering (chime)—both proper to verse; (3) performance (pitch, and a system of musical marks)—not integral to verse, though important in reading. The key words 'pitch' and 'stress' returned from visual uses to oral origins, for pitch was degree of tuning in the musical scale and stress the force of pulse-beat in rhythm.[1] Hopkins was teaching himself to play the piano, not for execution but for theory's sake (I. 30). When after several years he returned to verse theory for his lectures, he thought of verse as speech framed for music. Speech, verse, and music were becoming three levels of vocal utterance mutually enriched by correspondence. Now, since the law of the naturalistic ideal was inscape, the holding-fast of energetic shape to basic unity of being, verse became 'inscape of spoken sound' (IV. 249)—a dwelling upon figures of sound, sound repeated through variations to fasten them into a naturally developed pattern, yet a fixed type. If verse was inscape of spoken sound, music was inscape of pitched sound; poetry, verse heightened, was to be considered the virtue or *arete* of verse (IV. 250).

Verse then was to be speech recast as sound. Certainly rhythm was only one element in the sound pattern, though a vital one, for it conveyed the life-force of meaning through mimetic movement, whether rising (a forward motion of

40

present action suitable for drama), rocking (a complex combination of ups and downs suitable for lyric), or falling (a downward succession suiting narrative and epic). Total rhythmic flow in a stanza was important, from the foot, a rhythmic word, through the metre or bar, a rhythmic sub-clause, to the verse, a clause, and stanza, a sentence. Scanning was based on several possible factors, time (quantity), beat (accent), count (number); it was beat-rhythm, more particularly stress, which received Hopkins' attention (IV. 229–31, 233–5).

If rhythm was the unifying force of verse, its sound-curvature,[2] then chiming or lettering was the repetitive shape its power assumed: speech recast as inscape by calculation of syllable-by-syllable design. Alliteration, assonance, inner rhyme were devices of sound-colour and echo linking beginning, middle, and end-sounds of syllables. The vowel was most essential in giving melodic strain to the stress-beat, either by 'vowelling on' in echolalia, an example of Platonic 'shadow', or by 'vowelling off' in an alphabetic scale of vowels or in a distinct series of notes. Chiming on vowels gave to the verse 'brilliancy, starriness, quain, margaretting' (IV. 243, 251). Hopkins had previously associated starriness with 'the strong swell given by the deeper yellow middle' of primroses (IV. 143). 'Margaretting' would therefore be the weaving of vowels into a daisy-chain of notes; 'quain' would refer to the brilliant star-angled consonants used to square-in the shining vowels.

There were then two elements proper to verse: the rhythm, a continuous figure of energetic stress, and the lettering, an intermittent figure of chime. In so defining rhythm and chime Hopkins usefully extended his theory of two kinds of beauty set forth in the Platonic dialogue of 1865—chromatic or continuous, diatonic or abrupt.

Pitch, the third element, not integral to verse but giving beauty in reading, stood for the singing note or for intonation in general (IV. 223). Hopkins dismissed this element from formal consideration of verse: '*ring* or *tang* or *grain* (*timbre*) . . . personal or provincial etc accent; loudness and softness;

accent of meaning, logical, rhetorical, and ethical emphasis and intonation' (IV. 222). But he soon began to use a system of marks to regulate the rendition of his poetry—slurs, glides, pauses, breaks, stress marks, many of them based on musical notation. This development began in the revision of the poem on St. Dorothea (No. 25), where stress marks were introduced, and continued in the lecture on rhythm, where holding of syllables, usually of vowels, was denoted by break, circumflex, diphthong-mark (IV. 248). A scheme of Hopkins' marks is partially recoverable from the Bridges collection, Manuscript A, but it is incomplete. Hopkins never satisfied himself about the necessity of such marks. Though external to the verse proper, this third element, amounting to a musical scoring for performance, becomes of great concern to readers wishing to follow the poet's own intention, that his verse be read aloud and come alive to the ear.[3]

Hopkins' lectures included remarks on prose rhythm; he quoted Aristotle's preference for the paeon (to become a basic unit of sprung rhythm), for complexity of ratio between its stress and slack parts. As an example of oratory he cited the Asiatic school: his own undated translation of Chrysostom's Homily on the Fall of Eutropius was a fair illustration of what he wished rhythm in prose to be—periodic and flowing, hovering between random and metrical speech (IV. 232–3, 256–9). In a year of lecturing Hopkins' interest in art noticeably revived. He made visits to galleries and museums, noting inscapes and colour-chords in paintings, the red and blue-green scales of gems, the strings of musical instruments (IV. 183–4, 187–97): these notes show the perpetuation of his characteristic preoccupations in art—chromatic colour-music and diatonic type-shape, Platonic themes of the Pre-Raphaelite school. Hopkins was at last emerging from long mortification of his artistic genius, ready to use his poetic gift when a fitting opportunity would arise. With the wreck of the *Deutschland* in the Thames estuary in December 1875, the occasion arrived.

PART III. INCREASE 1875–1884

8. THEOLOGY OF STRESS

In the years of Jesuit training Hopkins' creative vision received spiritual and psychological development which deepened his artistic response to external nature as well as his religious response to the things of God. At St. Beuno's College, North Wales, he was full of bardic enthusiasm for Welsh verse, its systems of lettering or chime; he acquired the bardic signature 'Brân Maenefa'. The double enrichment of vision and of verse required an outlet. Build-up of resources made the outburst, after seven years' silence, complex and exciting. *The Wreck of the Deutschland* (No. 28), the great ode of 1876, celebrated not one occasion, the drowning of five sisters; nor two, that and the poet's religious vocation; but three, these and the sweeping strength of Triune Godhead redeeming creation through Son and Spirit. The scope was cosmological, yet sprang from the factual, from the afflictive experience of the two protagonists, poet and chief nun. The heroic death of five Franciscan nuns in exile from Protestant Germany and in storm at England's door meant for Hopkins a martyrdom suiting daughters of St. Francis and an omen for Protestant England. It was the courage and crying to Christ of the mother nun which most deeply touched Hopkins, awakening from within his own story of finding God. The calendar date, December 7 (eve of the feast of the immaculate conception, a doctrine vigorously defended by Hopkins' philosopher, the Franciscan Scotus), was taken as a sign of the nuns' sanctification; hence the dedication, 'To the happy [that is, blessed] memory of five Franciscan Nuns.'[1]

The first part celebrates God's mastery of the poet. Hopkins acknowledges God first as Creator under all creation, holding all things, binding him fast in being. In the wreck account the poet retraces his own soul's history under the Spirit's inspiration: 'Over again I feel thy finger and find thee' (stanza 1. 8). He recalls three moments of stress during Ignatian retreat, involving his conversion and vocation, and he is led to acknowledge God secondly as Redeemer. The first stress, pressure of grace, is afflictive—Christ in terrible aspect, storming the soul which is laced with the Spirit's fire; the second, response to grace, instress, is elective—the heart choosing Christ; the third stress, act of sacramental grace, is elevating—the heart flying home to God in the Blessed Sacrament. The second act, inspired by the Holy Ghost—the stem of affirmation which elects Christ: 'I did say yes' (stanza 2. 1)—is completed when the heart appeals from Christ's frowning judgement to his mercy in the Host; thus the soul swings from first to third act, from grace to grace. There is a vast difference between the soul before and the soul after the moment of free election fulfilled in communion: beforehand, man's mortal nature collapses to the fall of sin as sand in the hourglass of the night watch; after the reception of grace, he is suddenly fed from the gospel mount by a rope of water which sustains the well of the soul (stanza 4). The fastened creature which was undermined by sin is now upheld by redemptive stress, another pressure of grace. The poet turns to God the Son, both Creator and Redeemer, as Light incarnate shining in stars, storms, sunsets of nature. This current of stress in the universe, particular immanence, is the mystery of the incarnation in creation, which must be 'instressed, stressed' (stanza 5. 7)— received by inward faith and re-enacted by outward imitation. God's creative activity is not felt, but his redemptive activity is felt, for the incarnation 'rides time like riding a river' (stanza 6. 7):[2] creation carries the design of incarnation as the stem of stress in history. Hopkins believes with Scotus in Christ's eucharistic or sacramental Presence working in created nature since the beginning of time.[3] After the fall of man, the incarnation meant life-in-death for Christ: his birth into earthly life was already a death ('Warm-laid grave of a womb-life grey'— stanza 7. 3) and his death was a rebirth discharged through the passion. Only by sharing like afflictions with Christ can the heart reveal him. The moment of choice, like judgement through the eucharistic Presence, reveals men as they are: they have immediate spiritual 'taste' of God, who, a crushed fruit flushing souls with divine energy, is sweet to those who say *yes*, sour to those who deny Christ (stanza 8). By such necessary affliction as shipwreck, whereby paradoxically love is found,[4] the Holy Trinity masters human nature to say *yes*—either suddenly as St. Paul or gradually as St. Augustine, to whom by great light or vocal sound came Christ's call and human response in conversion.[5]

The story of grace wrung through private storm in Part I, of the heart flung from justice to mercy, from darkness to light, is analogous to the chronicle of public storm in Part II, of the heart flung on the higher level of martyrdom. The first stress is afflictive—death in storm. Death severing all bonds of nature leads to the binding of souls in God: there are no lasting roots in earth, but by the dragnet of God's mercy his Providence may be hoped to 'reeve in' those drowned at sea (stanzas 11–12). The storm of God, an infinite air sweeping into a whirlwind of hard flakes, drives a ship of souls aground on a sandbank—the false ship beaten down, its powers of propulsion and steerage gone (stanzas 13–14).[6] To emphasize that nature cannot redeem itself, Hopkins personifies false Hope turning into deathlike Despair, shows the attempt to attract rescue as vain (stanza 15), and recounts how the natural man, a brave sailor, is killed in trying to save passengers below—the unfixed type anticipating the true, holding form of Christ who will arrive to redeem the nuns: natural strings of being, 'braids of thew' and 'rope's end', do not hold fast enough (stanza 16). The poet, driven to acknowledge that 'They fought with God's cold' (stanza 17. 1), responds to the tall nun who recognizes the same Lord through storm.

The second stress is correspondence to grace. Now Hopkins examines the stem of stress carrying nature into grace, by a series of analyses of the situation within which the nun's 'grace of correspondence' to the passion is acting. The requisite for instress is deep sigh of aspiration, which in the mother nun comes from the heart of all nature in suffering; the poet is touched in his own 'mother of being in me, heart' (stanza 18. 4), where stress and instress are stored and released. The heart, though biased to sin, utters truth of deep feeling in tears. This response, joy in suffering, reveals the residual goodness of nature reaching out for God, of nature being re-created as the immaculate conception towards which the poem is moving. Beyond storm the nun has 'one fetch' or breath of aspiration, her ejaculation to Christ (stanza 19). Saints are made by Christ. He, Orion in glory, angelic Judge weighing souls, is weaving stormflakes into lily showers to crown his martyrs (stanza 21). The five sisters are grouped in a circle of hoods, a five-leaved token or cinquefoil, 'cipher of suffering Christ'—sign of the five stigmata which were received by their father Francis through vision of seraphic crucifix (stanzas 22–3). The nun holds the crucifix to her and calls, 'O Christ, Christ, come quickly' (stanza 24. 7–8).[7] Between the saint's call in death and Christ's rescue, the poet continues to question this aspiration made through the crucifix. Its inspiration is 'original Breath', the Holy Ghost; its inspirer, the 'body of lovely Death', Christ on the cross (stanza 25. 2 and 4). Did she wish for death to be with her lover Christ? Did she desire reward, a heavenly crown? Neither possibility reaches high enough; both are ultimately escapes from suffering. How high can the heart aspire, and what is its highest good? There is no rejection of suffering here, but rather complete acceptance of it by embracing the crucifix. The nun's 'fetch' is 'Other', other than avoidance of the passion; hers is a hidden cry of entire faith (stanzas 25–7).

Suddenly the third stress follows. The poet's meditation is interrupted. Christ astride the storm arrives as King and Judge to redeem his virgin-martyr (stanza 28).[8] What makes rebirth of nature in grace is response to insight, the heart set right by the 'single eye': so the nun interpreted the 'unshape-able' affliction by the shape of the passion, holding fast to

46

Christ, the 'Lovescape crucified', and was filled with light as St. Peter in his confession (stanza 29). The Word has been 'instressed' by faith and 'stressed' by imitation. One conception answers another: the conception of God in heart or mind is rewarded by renewal of nature in God, immaculate conception.[9] The nun is a second Mary; Christ can be saluted both in the Blessed Virgin and in the virgin souls uttering or giving birth to him (stanza 30). Other souls are to be prayed for 'at a bitterer vein' of grace; the finger of Providence will respond softly to intercessions; and there is hope that the harvest of death will gather God's grain (stanza 31).

The setting closes by returning to the thought of Part I: Being is affirmed in oneness under all, a re-creation sustaining unsteady waters of nature in flux—whether tides and the deluge, or seasons and man's mind (stanza 32). The ship is recovered in the heavenly dock; the soul is stanched from falling. God is not sand but 'granite', 'Ground of being', solid Reality. Death in nature is not absolute: 'past all | Grasp God, throned behind | Death' (stanza 32. 6–8). While God's justice waits, his mercy goes out, even under purgatory, the utmost mark Christ reached in his storm the passion (stanza 33). Christ is now reborn in another soul redeemed into the twofold centre of the Holy Trinity (stanza 34). The storm over, the poet turns to the sister in heaven and prays her to intercede for England's conversion, for the release of the shower of grace in light (stanza 35).

Verse inscape and sprung rhythm give the poem the pyrotechnics of song. Welsh lettering or *cynghanedd* enriches such lines as 'And frightful a nightfall folded rueful a day' (stanza 15. 5). Here a chain of stressed vowels ($\bar{\imath}, \bar{\imath}, \bar{o}, \bar{oo}, \bar{a}$) is interwoven with repetitive lighter vowels ($\breve{a}, \breve{u}, \breve{e}$) and consonants ($n, d, f, r, t, l$). But it is the theological application of inscape which should not be missed. Basic bonds of being are manifested by shaping of God's power or stress—the 'finger' of the Holy Ghost, the 'vein' sustaining the soul by a rope, the 'discharge' and current of grace riding the river of time, the dragnet of God's mercy set against natural roots and ropes, the 'vein' of prayer—until in the crucifix and the arrival of Christ's Presence the true type is revealed: God's inscape is 'Lovescape crucified', his seal the stigmata; and this is the real shape of 'the unshapeable shock night' which the nun words rightly by the Word himself.

Stress is the characteristic theme. The two actions of the ode are analogues of grace, but are one history in Christ—the poet flung to the Host, the nun rescued to the heaven-haven —each by the same sequence of stress: affliction/storm; election/aspiration; elevation/rescue. It is apparent in each case that Hopkins was fascinated by nature's response, by the middle term, the stem of stress in spiritual feeling which received affliction and instressed grace through the passion. The spiritual facts of the two actions were so closely associated in the poet's mind that in tracing out Part II he re-traced his own experience of Part I and kept breaking into the second action. There was a complication of stress—not only correspondence to Christ in poet and nun separately, but also heart-to-heart greeting in the communion of saints, the poet's response to the nun's response. This interaction generated the poem itself: 'make words break from me here all alone, | Do you!' (stanza 18. 3–4).

The two parts make one poem, in theme and character, in detail and symbol. Sand and water in the receptacle of the soul in Part I (stanza 4) become sandbank and ocean finally gathered into 'the recovery of the gulf's sides' in Part II (stanza 32). Properties of storm, night, fire are intensified in passing from I to II. In structure the two parts form parallel actions of stress within one encompassing action of Being, the Triune God. Now being has two words, inscape and instress. In Hopkins' theology of stress, the Father has Lovescape, Christ, and the fire Love itself, the Holy Ghost, the two processions within and outside the Godhead. Heartfelt sequence of stress corresponds to a theology of stress quite explicit in the ode: the affliction/storm is Christ's; the election/ aspiration is the heart's under the Spirit's inspiration; the elevation/rescue is Christ's. The Holy Ghost presides over the stem of stress bearing creation into the Godhead and over the incarnation of the Son in marian souls. Such is the fulfilment of Hopkins' twofold vision, witness of inscape and psychology of instress. The conversion of sensation to the uses of the spirit had thus been achieved. As forms were felt, inscapes gave instresses, Lovescape gave Love. The two Words of Being were the two Paracletes, Son and Spirit, calling on human nature to correspond to grace.

9. VISIONARY SENSATION

AT the close of his priestly training in Wales, Hopkins burst out in joyous verse, all of it experimental in rhythm, lettering, musical devices, as well as sacramental in thought and symbol. In Oxford verse the two worlds of flesh and spirit, earth and heaven, had been set against each other in choice and judgement. In the Jesuit verse the two worlds met by incarnational and sacramental vision. God's grace was working through nature, renewing creation to the unfallen condition of innocence, which was a shaming judgement on man in trade and town. This theme, very like Ruskin, was based on a number of fundamental insights: (1) resources of stress and instress, (2) nature's unfallen ideal, (3) expressions of variegated inscape, (4) fallen man. The life of spiritual feeling, of 'dearest freshness deep down things', was presided over by the brooding Holy Ghost who charged and discharged gathered 'greatness' of stress in the world (No. 31). The unfallen ideal, a blue air glassy and sheltering on earth, was nature innocent, summed up in Mary immaculate (Nos. 33, 60). 'Dappled things' casting off light and sound in twofold behaviour were effectual signs or sacramentals of Christ's divine-human natures; 'piece-brightness' provided glimpses of God's Light through sparks of creation; 'meal-drift' showed God's eucharistic grain in cloud and field; and all creation aspired to express the ideal human nature of Christ (Nos. 37, 32, 38). Man, the rebel of the *Deutschland*, was, however, seldom in character to correspond to such grace as nature carried to him; he was a caged skylark in moods, a labourer soiled with toil, an inhabitant of the industrial town (Nos. 39, 31, 35).

The vision was achieved through sensation spiritualized. Hopkins had exercised Ignatian and Scotist techniques of sensation—the application of the senses to holy things for spiritual ends, from St. Ignatius; the holding and flowering of sensation below conscious thought, from Duns Scotus.[1]

50

Hopkins verified his own intuitive experience when he learned from Scotus, that sensation in breaking from the unconscious was still vaguely identified with being in general, and that it could be held below fully conscious thought to give intuition of being. The moment of visionary sensation was so fleeting that it had somehow to be 'caught' or 'stalled'. In waking from sleep the leap from unconscious to conscious awareness was slowed down to a gradual process of unfolding. *Moonrise* (No. 99) presented such a vision upon waking:

> This was the prized, the desirable sight, | unsought, presented
>   so easily,
> Parted me leaf and leaf, divided me, | eyelid and eyelid of
>   slumber.

The soul, a sheaf of faculties, was folded in sleep, but opened itself into distinct activities, 'leaf and leaf' in waking. Simple being was common to both infinite God and his finite creatures; the vague intuition of God through his creation was achieved on a level of mind below rational and abstractive thought. If primitive sensation were held to, then sight led to insight, evoking response in the heart. The senses had to be fastened, abstractive thought avoided: sensations had to dig firmly into the senses ('two noises . . . | Trench', No. 35) and the mind had to stall, hold in position, the sensations ('I caught', No. 36). Piercing and penetrative sights and sounds struck deep and pure, while the mind receiving sensations intensified or 'fixed' them in actions—expressed by such verbs as 'look', 'see', 'catch', 'lift'. There was another set of verbs for the subsequent dedication of sensations to God—the instressing of sensation —'buy' and 'bid', 'have' and 'get', 'stir' and buckle', 'glean' and 'hurl' (Nos. 32, 33, 36, 38). These verbs show how Hopkins held to Ignatian application of sensation. In the *Spiritual Exercises* the retreatant was to imagine a scene of sacred story, to apply each of the senses in turn, and to draw out personal and moral lessons thereby. In the sacramental sonnets Hopkins made use of sonnet divisions—an octave of two quatrains and a sestet of two tercets—by pivoting in argument through affective and didactic turns, much as

Ignatian meditation must have its fruits in colloquies and resolutions of prayer.

The soul was a sheaf of faculties; in the Augustinian tradition followed by St. Ignatius these were memory, understanding, and will, basic activities harnessed for meditation in the Ignatian method. Now Hopkins, wishing to achieve intuition of being below the level of abstractive understanding, used in his poetry the characteristic sequence of sensation, intuition, and response. By understanding the rational level he could respond to vision by spontaneous acts of will. So would appear that in prayer Hopkins had passed from discursive considerations to affective acts, and the change influenced his poetry. Passage from sensation to intuition was often instantaneous: a shape was caught in curved oneness as inscape, stress was felt, and subsequent acts of instress followed rapidly, turning the message of inscape to spiritual profit. Insight and response revolve in *Hurrahing in Harvest* (No. 38). Visionary sensation and affective willing join in greeting Christ of eucharistic grain in harvest field and cloudy sky—'I lift up heart, eyes', 'And, eyes, heart'—the sequence turning upon itself. Christ's face is gleaned from cloudy sky, his shoulder from blue hills. Once this incarnational inscape in the object is met by a sensing subject, 'The heart rears wings': the will responds spontaneously in affective acts, growing those spiritual wings in response to beauty which Plato had described.[2]

Hopkins' acts of will were extended by ability to feel stress, to aspire, and to instress. The principal verbs of *The Windhover* (No. 36) clarify this extension, already found in the stress-theology of the *Deutschland*. The sequence is marked out by syntax: (1) 'I caught' an inscape at full stress, a royal bird parading as the *anima Christi* in flight and turn; (2) 'My heart . . . | Stirred for a bird', desired to imitate, sighed from inscape to incarnation, to Christ; then (3), with change to imperative mood and present tense, physical qualities of the falcon are spiritualized, instressed, in one act of sacrificial offering of powers to Christ—'here | Buckle!'[3] Christ, the

52

Prince of Light, reigning in the windhover as in his proper realm of spirit,[4] shines at dawn from the East of resurrection. Within this glorious field the bird's actions are connected to the source by lines of being: 'dapple-dawn-*drawn*', 'rung upon the *rein*', 'on *swing*', 'on a *bow-bend*'. By wavering lines the stress of Christ so informs the natural inscape that it becomes virtually his tremendous spirit courageous in the passion, showing his mastery of suffering. Hopkins was not only transcribing the Ignatian meditation on the kingdom of Christ, but also in part representing the Ignatian prayer, the *Anima Christi*.[5] The poet's 'heart in hiding' is hid in the holy wounds, hid with Christ in God, trusting the Saviour to rebuff 'the big wind' of the malicious enemy, crying to be more closely joined to the passion. Christ then acts in the heart: after his armour is buckled on, his fire of sacrifice draws wounds that break out in shining soil or gashed coals on the field or hearth of the heart.[6] There are four parallel terms in the sonnet: as the bird rides the windy air or as a knight strides his reined steed, so the spirit of Christ is to be buckled onto the soul and the cross-plough to turn up furrows in the soil of the heart.[7]

The sequence of subjective acts—sensation held to give intuition followed by response of instress—was directed to an objective vision of creation. The elements of vision were seen as active essences of being, according to the Platonist tradition of St. Augustine and the Franciscans: the ascending ladder of nature anticipated God in ever intenser degrees, all summed up as ideas in God's Word, Archetype of creation.[8] In Hopkins' verse, elements of fire, air, earth, and water, caught by visionary sensation at moments of breaking with deep inscapes, acquired spiritual direction, sacramentalization. Natural light, water, sound were activated into holy fires, saps, songs.[9] Light no longer passed into physical colour merely, but struck a deeper level of spiritual intensity, fire, and by flaming out in excited stars, creased foil, firecoals, leaved flares, appeared to be the jewels and very eyes of God's sanctuary. The sky in *The Starlight Night* (No. 32) became, in rapid succession, a heavenly city of lights, an earthly mine of diamonds, a windblown tree of leaves, in which dwelt folk, elves, doves. The vision was summed up in orchard blossoms, for sale to the proper bidder of prayer. Natural beauties bought for Christ were supernaturalized into his harvest home. Chains of analogy fell into place, all fiery lights into one frame: 'This piece-bright paling shuts the spouse | Christ home, Christ and his mother and all his hallows.' The element of water too was intensified—squeezed into biblical oil and wine, milk and honey, saps and liquors enriching the taste of nature with God. Richness rushed down the sky; freshness lived down the earth. In the *Deutschland* this flush or gush was the current of grace released at the passion; in sonnets of 1877 Hopkins was considering the current of grace in original or ideal nature of unfallen Eden.

The elements were not isolated, but creatively mingled in dealing out one another—fire and water, water and air. Fire and water were combined in the sense of sight. In *The Lantern out of Doors* (No. 34) Hopkins adapted the Empedoclean doctrine of sight by which the eye was a lantern of fire in water and sight a physical thread or effluence between eye and object.[10] In the sonnet the lantern is external beauty, 'out of doors', a fire sending beams through water-thick air, attracting eyebeams to follow by stem of interest. In the octave the lantern sends out 'wading light' and beauties 'rain' beams; in the sestet the eye can 'wind after' these beautiful objects. Rather than physical eyebeams, Hopkins thought of definite interest, stem of stress, leading a subject to follow the devious course of an object (I. 66–7). In hearing, air and water made the mingled medium: 'thrush | . . . does so rinse and wring | The ear, [now joined to spiritual fire] it strikes like lightnings to hear him sing' (No. 33). *The Sea and the Skylark* (No. 35) illustrates nature's vocal renewals through rise and fall of water in air—tide ramping horizontally under the moon's control; lark winding, unwinding, rewinding a vertical skein of liquid song from and upon a winch. It should be noted that threads of interest—strings of song, reins of falcon drawn to

Christ, winding of eye—were the vehicles of stemming stress, whether in inscaped object, between object and subject, or between inscape and another part of its field. Sometimes the connecting link was a line or curve; at other times, only a breath aspiring to form a chain. Such were tokens which energized the vision.

While objective vision and subjective acts were joined in the sacramental sonnets, versification took on a mimetic character by virtue of expressive rhythm and lettering. Hopkins interwove poems by roving over end-rhymes and by scanning a stanza from beginning to end—an organic curvature suiting a vision of linked being. He employed a series of techniques to freshen verse through stress: (1) standard rhythm counterpointed, (2) sprung rhythm, (3) sprung rhythm outriding. Counterpoint added the interest of a second rhythm 'mounted' on the standard. Sprung rhythm exploited a fuller range of effects, rising, rocking, falling. Sensations of floating, wavering, sinking could thus be imitated by stress and slack in rhythm, often a characteristic springing energy. Beyond counterpoint and sprung rhythm, Hopkins devised an extrametrical foot, the outride, which hovered outside the metre, somewhat as his own vision hovered between worlds and as the sigh of correspondence hovered between stress and instress. In two sonnets sprung and outriding, *The Windhover* (No. 36) and *Hurrahing in Harvest* (No. 38), both greeting Christ in inscape, Hopkins used the outride to charge the rhythm with free flights and with sighs of feeling. In *The Woodlark* (No. 100) he imitated the bird's spontaneous trickle of song by variable stress with or without slack or pause—

> I am so very, O so very glad
> That I do think there is not to be had . . .
> Of a sweet—a sweet—sweet—joy—

to reconstruct an infectious sequence of trill, gush, purl, and other birdlike strains. Such naturalistic verse, especially the mimetic instinct of repeating the same sound in chime, was release of emotion in poetry, catharsis—a Romantic principle taken into religious verse by such a poet-critic as Keble.[11]

Lettering by assonance and consonance between adjacent words—'blood-gush blade gash'—had been exploited in the *Deutschland* according to Welsh and pseudo-Welsh harmonies.[12] Chime, vowelling on and off, was Hopkins' speciality. The most remarkable example was *The Windhover* (No. 36), scored for several vowels, each with high and low variants, like a sharp above and a flat below the note. The musical strain was woven or 'margaretted' into bell-changes, rung on a rein through a few vowels at a time in alphabetic or broken sequences. Chime and stress together accounted for expressive imitations in sound-value alone of ecstatic climb, majestic turn, sacrificial plunge.

10. MOULD AND HEART OF MAN

DURING five years of active priesthood in England Hopkins' attention was taken up with duties of urban parishes and directed to the cure of souls. His vision of creation, which had developed from observation of external nature, now turned to man and man's spiritual condition. The earlier theme of nature's unfallen ideal set against fallen man came out again in certain sonnets in which man did not correspond to 'cordial air', 'sweet earth', and 'rural keeping' (Nos. 40, 58, 44). Creation thus judged man. In addition, it anticipated redemption and displayed the way to Christ through Mary: in the joy of spring there were the red of Christ's sacrifice and the blue of Mary's purity—'drop-of-blood-and-foam-dapple | Bloom' and 'azuring-over greybell makes | . . . wash wet like lakes' (No. 42): in the wild, blue atmosphere of Mary there was mercy to let Christ through (No. 60). The naturalistic ideal anticipated and pointed man to the Humanity of Christ. The ideal for man was imitation of Christ by dedication, obedience, service—in a word, sacrifice, the type of which was the passion of our Lord. In turning to men for signs of such sacrifice, Hopkins found them in lives of devoted service, in soldiers, sailors, hardy men, whose physical discipline and moral duty were analogues of religious obedience.

The equivalent in man of natural inscape was 'manly mould'; its ideal was Christ. Human inscapes or moulds were to be prized. Loss of human inscapes was much worse than loss of natural ones, for souls were involved. The hewing down of trees—inscapes holding instress as 'airy cages' holding 'leaping sun'—was bad enough; so closely involved were object and subject in the vision of inscape that this violent action was equivalent to blinding the eye itself (No. 43). Now, in *The Loss of the Eurydice* (No. 41), the felling of human trees, 'hearts of oak', British sailors, involved a worse threat, 'The riving off' of souls from the Church. Hopkins found the loss tragic in a young corpse of 'manly mould', never to actualize complete form:

> Look, foot to forelock, how all things suit! he
> Is strung by duty, is strained to beauty . . .
>
> O his nimble finger, his gnarled grip!
> Leagues, leagues of seamanship
>   Slumber in these forsaken
> Bones, this sinew, and will not waken. (ll. 77–8, 81–4)

A being at tension, all strings on the strain, was a sign of service, of action from the will, of grasping and holding to a job. 'Give', 'hold', 'offer' were Hopkins' imperatives to fasten men to the true ideal, the Humanity of Christ (No. 48). The holding could not relax because the mainspring of evil, like a watch wound up in man, threatened to go; this coil or spiral was a type of the Devil (IV. 268, 346). Industrial man, heir of creation, was 'To his own selfbent so bound, so tied to his turn' (No. 58). And the young bugler, though communicated, 'may he not rankle and roam | In backwheels though bound home?' (No. 47). Man was in tension between the bond to himself and the bond to God.

If men were in a scale of being constantly dragging to a mainspring of evil, they had to brace themselves to the moral ideal of the true inscape. They could be fastened in position by Christ. God himself was 'Low-latched' in the Blessed Sacrament, in order to 'lock' love into the members of his Body the Church (No. 47). Christ had the key of sacrifice to lock men into the holding latch, his eternal ideal of resurrected and glorified human inscape. *The Leaden Echo* asked after that key or fixed type, and *The Golden Echo* gave the answer, in an orchestration of sound- and word-play (No. 59):[1]

How to keep—is there any any, is there none such, nowhere known
    some, bow or brooch or braid or brace, lace, latch or catch or
    key to keep
Back beauty, keep it, beauty, beauty, beauty, . . . from vanishing
    away? . .

Mould and Heart of Man

Yes I can tell such a key, I do know such a place,
Where whatever's prized and passes of us, . . .
Never fleets more, fastened with the tenderest truth
To its own best being and its loveliness of youth. . . .
Give beauty back, beauty, beauty, beauty, back to God, beauty's
    self and beauty's giver.

Now the search for a specific locking type to keep physical beauty from dying away in flux was a search for physical things through the metaphysical world of forms or ideas.[2] The outcome of the search was hinted at as 'to abstain', the meaning of 'to keep back'. The key itself had to do with the secret of Christ, the form of the servant (Philippians ii. 5–11), as explained by Hopkins: 'It is this holding of himself back, and not snatching at . . . the good that was his right, . . . which seems to me the root of all holiness and the imitation of this the root of all moral good in other men' (I. 175). Christ then by his life of incarnation and atonement had the true key, sacrifice. Physical beauty was to be kept back, abstained from, freely offered to God, held to an eternal youth of the spirit—how? by being fastened to its resurrection body, the true inscape in Christ, spiritual beauty. The poet played on key words and sounds through repeated figures, weaving and unweaving phrasal curves. The wavering motions expressed emotion, especially sighs of aspiration preceding dedication— 'And with sighs soaring, soaring sighs'. The double ode was Hopkins' Christian answer to the Cyrenaicism of the Conclusion to Pater's *Studies in the History of the Renaissance* (1873).

As the equivalent in man of inscape was 'mould' completed by sacrifice, so the equivalent of instress was 'heart' fulfilled in flight of dedication. The completed mould of mature man, both in body and in character, was the result of formative choices made by will or heart. So the mature mould 'big-boned and hardy-handsome' of Felix Randal had been hammered into shape 'at the random grim forge' of spontaneous will in youth, though in sickness 'a heavenlier heart' was fostered through priestly ministrations (No. 53). So the right choice

59

of a child, handsome-hearted in handsome 'case', required constant bracing against the backsliding tug of sin to go forward in the race of life and form good in the moral character (No. 51). Natural or spontaneous response of heart—'To its own fine function, wild and self-instressed', or 'to its well-being of a self-wise self-will'—was a wonder of youth to be greeted, encouraged, acknowledged, but it was not enough to guard against sin; so Hopkins turned to exhortation and intercession—'O brace sterner that strain!' and intercessory assault on 'adamantine heaven' (Nos. 51, 47).

Now there were levels of instress in the human heart or soul: on the level of mere feeling the heart responded by physical release in tears and song; on the level of winged spirit it responded by spiritual direction in flight; between the two, there was aspiration in sighs.[3] Tears entered into Hopkins' verse, particularly when, in spare time away from parochial duties, he wrote, out of simple release of feeling, weeping poems characteristic of a 'man of feeling'—'O well wept', 'I to him turn with tears', 'Thy tears that touched my heart', 'His tear-tricked cheeks of flame', 'And yet you will weep and know why' (Nos. 41, 52, 53, 54, 55). Joyful cries of feeling were discharged from the heart by songbirds, lark and cuckoo, in echoing figures 'flushing' the landscape (Nos. 42, 100, 108). However, there was a higher heart of power desiring to breathe and poise in air, to fly home to God. Spiritual direction and character were indicated by birds of flight and their wings. A carrier pigeon with true homing instinct stood for a young spirit spontaneously choosing good (No. 51). Birds of flight were to be distinguished in spiritual work from birds of song with mere cheevio or coo: so the 'wild wood-dove', Peace, 'comes with work to do, he does not come to coo' (No. 46). Birds mastering wind and storm—windhover and stormfowl (Nos. 36, 45)—were the most heroic spirits, like angels and archangels. Another symbol of strong spirit was the Platonic figure of horse and rider: the Captain of the *Eurydice* following his charge or charger, an intercessor riding a chariot of forward prayer 'with ride and jar', a farrier fettling a drayhorse, a brook 'horseback brown' on the highroad (Nos. 41, 47, 53, 56). Mastery of spirit meant courage, power, dominion, indicated by the characteristic word-image 'ride', expressing control over lower elements—as the incarnation 'rides time like riding a river', or the imperative of the Saviour, 'Let him ride . . . in his triumph', or the windhover 'riding | Of the rolling level underneath him steady air' (Nos. 28, stanzas 6 and 28; 36). The gaining of mastery was a tough struggle, a moral bracing to a task.

In picturing spiritual motions as flight of bird and riding of horse, Hopkins was relying upon Plato's famous myth of the tripartite soul whose functions of reason, spirit, appetite (*logos, thymos, epithymos*) were represented by a charioteer driving two winged horses, one noble, the other wild; the winged control of *thymos* was steady, the flight of *epithymos* untamed, erratic.[4] This myth is relevant to Hopkins' poem *The Brothers* (No. 54), in which the priest played the role of reason to higher and lower hearts in the two brothers—Jack, spirited young actor, courageous in mastering a stage role; Harry, older, 'heart-forsook' spectator, yielding to sympathetic feeling in tears off-stage. There were both the action of the main play and a little passion or suffering of 'byplay' in the audience. There was natural truth of feeling in the episode, sentimental as it was, for it showed response to a tug on the heart-strings, a genuine bond called 'love-lace': instress of feeling responded to stress on the reins of being. The active heart had heroic virtues, but the passive heart was private and domestic. Hopkins looked both to the heroic conduct of external action and to the humble lot of internal service, often in sequence from outward vision to inward application. So he called home his eye from the candle of a night worker to his own heart's candle: 'your fading fire | Mend first' (No. 50).[5] Thus, while human inscape strained into being through choice and could be locked into eternity through the key of sacrifice, human instress had different levels of response from release of feeling to elevating flight of spirit.

The higher and lower heart in music were represented by

61

Hopkins' favourites, Purcell in spirit, von Weber in feeling
(I. 98). Hopkins never tired of hearing and praising Purcell.
His sonnet *Henry Purcell* (No. 45) in sprung Alexandrines
developed ideas of human inscape and instress. He praised
the composer beyond mood or mere feeling for great genius
and for inscape. The genius or controlling spirit of Purcell
was portrayed as *thymos*—'so archangelic a spirit as heaves
in Henry Purcell,' an archangelic type expressing 'the very
make' or creative form of mankind,[6] and he went on to
represent this genius by a fitting heroic simile of 'some great
stormfowl' walking 'The thunder-purple seabeach' and raising
colossal wings. The inscape in Purcell's music was the uttering
of 'the very make and species of man so created both in him
and in all men generally', for an inscape was a specific type of
creation.[7] The inscape of sound uttered then both mankind
and Purcell; so the white-purple bird, lifting wings to soar in
control of thunderstorm, revealed its own quaintly marked
plumage, its 'sakes' or distinctive markings.[8] From this sonnet
the reader learns that inscape was a 'forgèd feature', often
repetitive or echoing, representing a species. It was also one
thing, an 'abrupt self', springing with unitive life of its own,
its 'thisness', what Scotus called *haecceitas*.[9] Because the
artist was a species to himself, he was distinctive; the inscape
of his art bore the stamp of his own unity of being. Hopkins
expressly denied the Romantic atomism of personality in art:
'My sonnet means "Purcell's music is none of your d—d
subjective rot" (so to speak)' (I. 84). Inscape was objective
essence fastened in concrete type. The artist was necessarily
though accidentally in his art.

What Hopkins found as mould of inscape and heart of
moulding instress in humanity corresponded in poetry to
rhetoric, the formal mechanics of verse design, and insight or
inspiration, the informing impulse of creation. In correspondence with three friends and fellow-poets, Bridges, Dixon,
Patmore, Hopkins used as critical touchstones his familiar
concepts of inscape and instress, coining terms, 'sequence of
phrase' and 'sequence of feeling', to stand for two sorts of

artistic excellence which Bridges' verse possessed (II. 8).
What English verse lacked, in spite of all its inspiration, was
a sound rhetoric. Here Milton was the great master of 'sequence
of phrase', the standard for English verse; almost all other
poets were licentious in some degree. Hopkins invariably
suggested improvements in the rhetoric of his friends' verses,
although he took pains to commend their inspiration: Bridges
had a rare character, a true humanity of spirit, and Dixon,
deep pathos, tragic feeling, primitive and pure imagination[10]
—qualities of higher and lower heart respectively. While
Hopkins was establishing his rhetorical standards—for
counter-point, Milton in blank verse and choric drama, Ovid
in elegiac couplet, Horace in Sapphic and Alcaic stanzas (II.
15, 25)—he was defending his admiration for unadorned
instress, such as in the west-country spontaneity of the
dialect poet William Barnes (I. 87–8). But in his own case he
could not in conscience devote time to poetry, when inspiration failed and rhetoric became difficult, time-consuming
work:

> Feeling, love in particular, is the great moving power and spring
> of verse and the only person that I am in love with seldom,
> especially now, stirs my heart sensibly and when he does I cannot
> always 'make capital' of it, it would be a sacrilege to do so. Then
> again I have of myself made verse so laborious. (I. 66)

Here the reader finds an explicit connexion between consolation in prayer and inspiration in poetry. When spontaneous
ejaculations and affective acts became infrequent, then the
poetic vision of sacramentalism lost its edge and zest. A new
kind of prayer and a new venture of art were needed. So forced
acts in the dry will and experimentation in music were soon
to follow in Hopkins' experience.

11. NATURE, PITCH, AND WILL

HOPKINS' Platonic Realism, the basis for his theory of inscape and instress, had been developed at Oxford from a philosophy of beauty to a metaphysics or science of being. Later, through a Scotist reading of Ignatian experience, there came in verse, in the *Deutschland* ode, the first mature exposition of his thought, an artist's vision of Triune Being redeeming creation. And further, in the years after his ordination, Hopkins, continuing to meditate upon the great mysteries, entered Scotist notes (dated 1878–85) in the interleaves of his Roothaan edition of the *Exercitia Spiritualia*. During his tertianship at Roehampton (1881–2) he thought seriously of a commentary; he copied out a rough draft for the Provincial before leaving Roehampton (I. 150). Only the notes are extant: they show clearly that Hopkins was extending his shaping vision into a cosmological scheme of salvation. The notes were to become as central to his thought and poetry after 1878 as the Oxford essays and early Greek studies had been to his previous work. While in the notes the ideas of inscape and instress were reapplied to philosophical and religious problems, the ideas of nature, self, and will were to the fore, along with the key word 'pitch'. Questions of providence and free will had already entered the two odes on shipwreck (Nos. 28, 41), and spiritual response to grace had become a favourite theme. Now, in fragmentary comments on the *Exercises*, activities of grace and will came to dominate his thought.

Hopkins' doctrine of the self took time to mature. He had relied upon the prefix 'in-' to denote interior unity in the two related words of being, inscape and instress, but he had not immediately examined unity or oneness in itself, to discover what made each creature fixed as a singular, an individual. It eventually became apparent that singularity was a crucial concept for which he must find an explanation and a specific

64

word. Among the first notes of the *Exercises* (1880) there was
an examination of this oneness called 'selfbeing' with determination called 'pitch'—individual degree in the tonal scale
of being—roughly equivalent to Scotus' *haecceitas*, 'thisness',
the fulfilment of individual degree (IV. 328).[1] Creation of
distinctive selves in the world of nature or universal being
could be due, neither to chance nor to self-existence, but only
to some extrinsic power, the power of the universal, the Self
of Being, God (IV. 309–17). What made anything one individual thing was pre-established by God as its pitch, its
fixed point in relation to a whole scale of such degrees. A self
consisted of a centre and a surrounding area, a point of reference and a belonging field (IV. 315). In later notes Hopkins
more closely defined the concept: self, intrinsic oneness of a
thing, was prior to its being: the centre or bare self before
nature was only possible, while with the accession of nature
overlaid it became truly a self (IV. 322, 325, 328).

The Scotist opposition between nature and individuality
(self) with respect to the creature, based on the distinction
between mind and will in God, became central to Hopkins'
thought, as in the following fragment:

What being in rank-old nature should earlier have that breath been
That hére pérsonal tells off these heart-song powerful peals?
                                                    (No. 101)

Upon hearing spirited music, Hopkins wondered what its
selfbeing would have been at a more primitive level of the
common nature. The breath or *thymos*, if separated from the
personal level of human reason, might have assumed the
nature of a frowning billow, ocean curvature, thundering
ashore under windblown storm and tide—yet 'seen | Under-
neath, their glassy barrel, of a fairy green', glimpsed in origin
as ideal. In the *Deutschland* too, nature was stormy air and
sea, raw matter, reaching out for a redeeming and completing
self in the Person of Christ; nature came to its eye and tongue
in the chief nun, who interpreted the labour of nature aright
by the Word of God.

For Scotus the act of creation had three moments. (1) God

had the idea of nature in his mind; here an idea was fixed as a perfect species imitating the divine essence from which it was not yet separated. All ideas or species were summed up in the Word. (2) God equipped nature with individuality in his will; here a species was supplied with power of self-determination, pitch, individual direction, still prior to existence. All degrees of individuality were summed up in the Humanity of Christ. (3) Nature and individuality combined in execution, embodying the idea of (1) and the grace of (2); here the world of actual existence entered. There were (1) a world of possibles in God's mind and (2) a world of intentions in his will; what was already real to God was made real to man by (3) co-operation with his will.

So Hopkins found creation as threefold act:

For in the world, besides natures or essences or 'inscapes' and the selves, supposits, hypostases, or, in the case of rational natures, persons | which wear and 'fetch' or instance them, there is still something else—fact or fate. (IV. 322)

There were then three terms in Hopkins' metaphysics: (1) nature (shapes, species, inscapes), (2) individuality (selves, pitches), (3) will (existential instress) together with access of grace (stress). Pitch gave single degree or unified direction of intensity to an idea. Overlaid nature provided the vessel or vehicle through which pitch could act. (In man, human nature supplied reason, so that the self of a man became a person.) Free will, residing in pitch and nature, actualized one course of action from a field of possible courses. The relationships among all these concepts were worked out by Hopkins through a musical figure: nature was scaled in degrees or levels; dynamics of the scale depended on the absolute will of God and on the free will of the creature. If self were taken to be the basic fibre of being, then pitch would be the degree of tuning of its string before a note were played upon it; the notes played by God would be stresses of grace and those by the self would be instresses of will; the pattern of the notes designed by God would be inscape.

The poetic exegesis of this philosophy of nature, pitch, and will came in a private sonnet of 1884–5, *Spelt from Sibyl's Leaves* (No. 62), 'the longest sonnet ever made and no doubt the longest making' (I. 245). Evening, the shadow of earth in the angelic sphere, is possible creation, privation of being reaching out for fullness of being. This primitive world of the heavens, straining to encompass total creation, the tomb-womb of night, is Eve unredeemed attempting to become Mary redeemed, and she is therefore adorned with the apocalyptic emblems of the Virgin (Revelation xii): a mock sun for the crescent moon ('fond yellow hornlight'), Northern Lights for sun-clothing ('wild hollow hoarlight'), a few chief stars for the complete crown of twelve ('earl-stars, stars principal'). This is a sign of the End, of death and judgement. On the last day, earth, actual creation, disintegrates: the corruption is a literal 'throwing-together' ('as- | tray or aswarm, all throughther, in throngs'). The strings of being are 'unbound'. Selves are torn from their natures, intensified in themselves ('steepèd'), losing reason ('Disremembering') and body ('dis-membering'). The cosmological vision of heaven and earth is interpreted by the will ('Heart') as a warning to root out personal sin ('beak-leaved boughs dragonish').[2] Life's twofold thread of good and evil is to be wound off, reeled into heaven and hell; the fibres of being are strung on a rack of torture, thoughts ground into groans. This poem, written when Hopkins' cosmological scheme in the commentary was rejected by his Jesuit superiors, displays both the visionary system and its personal application to a mind now in torment.

In addition to nature and pitch in Hopkins' spiritual universe, there was will; it was here that he had come to grief in metaphysical speculation. Will was for him the soul's energy all the way from root feelings and desires to higher powers and intentions. He was already distinguishing moments or instresses of will on different levels, higher and lower heart, in his poetry. Now in prose notes he drew a more exact, different yet analogous, distinction between two states of will, active and passive: *arbitrium* was will at pitch, deciding action; *voluntas* was will at splay, affected well or ill

67

towards things—later to be called elective and affective will
(IV. 317, 326–7).[3] Ever since the *Deutschland* Hopkins had
been attempting to formulate spiritual activities, but he had
only instress available as a word to express moments of will.
Now, by application of the Scotist opposition between nature
and individuality, he went further: *arbitrium*, will at pitch,
was independent of nature, free, while *voluntas*, will relaxed,
was determined by nature, not free (IV. 326). The pitched will
was braced or buckled to moral discipline—hence, in the
poetry, the military imagery of battle. The relaxed will acted
by natural spontaneity—hence, in the poetry, the organic
imagery of growth. It was the higher will, will beyond
nature, will as pitch on its own, that Hopkins eventually
thought made free moral choices (in man, will beyond rational
nature!). Hopkins dramatized the two states of will in
Caradoc's soliloquy (No. 105, Act II of *St. Winefred's Well*).
Caradoc was overly well affected towards Winefred, and,
when she would not submit to his lust, he elected to behead
her. By his violent deed he cut off (1) the martyr's head, (2)
the object of his affections, (3) his subject-nature with his
own affections:

I all my being have hacked | in half with her neck: one part,
Reason, selfdisposal, | choice of better or worse way,
Is corpse now, cannot change; | my other self, this soul,
Life's quick, this kind, this keen self-feeling, . . .
Must all day long taste murder. | What do now then? Do? Nay,
Deed-bound I am; one deed treads all down here | cramps all doing.
     What do? Not yield,
Not hope, not pray; despair; | ay, that: brazen despair out,
Brave all, and take what comes. . . . (ll. 60–3, 65–8)

Reason and affective will were dead. The murderer was left
with his other self, forever bound by elective will to the deed
not repented of. Stem of stress between object and subject had
been cut, and both were injured.[4] The only bond left was that
to self, the will at pitch of evil.

     Besides selving and activity of will, freedom of will was a
major concern of Hopkins. To get at a theory of free will, he

postulated three freedoms. Choice of will depended upon subject (self and nature) and object: in the subject the self supplied determination, pitch, and the nature supplied exercise, play; the object supplied the field of choice. There were, therefore, (1) freedom of pitch in the chooser, (2) freedom of play in the execution, (3) freedom of field in the object of choice; and free will properly consisted in the first two (IV. 323, 326).[5] Hopkins applied this theory of free will to art in *On a Piece of Music* (No. 110), in which the poet searched musical composition for the true self of the composer, his basic freedom:

> Not free in this because
> His powers seemed free to play:
> He swept what scope he was
> To sweep and must obey.
>
> Though down his being's bent
> Like air he changed in choice,
> That was an instrument
> Which overvaulted voice.

The basic freedom of music was not in the performer who, supplying execution (freedom of play), had to obey the original notation or 'scope' of the art-work;[6] nor in the instrument which, supplying the object (freedom of field), 'overvaulted voice' or subject; but the basic freedom was in the composer himself, 'his being's bent' or bias of pitch, his free choice. Hopkins went on to maintain that the good of the music was instinctive goodness, independent of moral choice of right or wrong, independent of *arbitrium*. The perfect song expressing the species was morally neutral, coming from the *voluntas naturae*. Yet the making of the mature man was in the *arbitrium*, in the instressing of service to God or to Satan:

> What makes the man and what
> The man within that makes:
> Ask whom he serves or not
> Serves and what side he takes.

While artistic inscape from the spontaneous will was 'wild' or innocent of moral values—like musical and colour-scales, like instincts of birds and bees—human character from the will braced at pitch did involve moral absolutes.

Hopkins gave full poetic expression to his concept of pitch in the sonnet 'As kingfishers catch fire' (No. 57). Here he was concerned with what he called in notes the 'doing-be' (IV. 328), the Scotist *praxis*, the positing or pitching of the whole self in personal act of will:

> As kingfishers catch fire, dragonflies draw flame;
> As tumbled over rim in roundy wells
> Stones ring; like each tucked string tells, each hung bell's
> Bow swung finds tongue to fling out broad its name;
> Each mortal thing does one thing and the same:
> Deals out that being indoors each one dwells;
> Selves—goes itself; *myself* it speaks and spells;
> Crying *Whát I dó is me: for that I came.*

All degrees in nature reach out to utter self in willed activity. Self-willed tension or selving at any degree in the scale is uttered to be answered by doing, as pitch in being gives instress in activity. One type answers another. Hence, kingfishers flash to feed on dragonflies in a moment of exchanged fire; stones tumble into wells at a moment of ringing—both showing forth reflexion or echo.[7] Furthermore this echo in doing displays the identity of inner being, as the resonance of a plucked string, or as the identifying note or name of a swung bell. Though pitch is prior to the exercise of its nature, though the idea is prior to its existential wholeness, in the Platonist and Scotist order,[8] yet the self truly comes into being only with the accession of nature in action: 'Selves—goes itself.' Then, in a turn from selving of being in the octave to the Self to which universal being aspires in the sestet, the poet goes goes on to selving in human nature: 'the just man justices; | Keeps grace . . .| Acts . . . '| Christ'. A man is not justified in external action but in internal being. Whoever acts in Christ-like manner so acts because first Christ through grace is in him. True selving follows God's will which is completed in the

70

Humanity of Christ, for Christ sums up all the individual degrees of nature. The sonnet thus completes the doing-be of self-revelation in Christ, the Stem of stress between individual selves of universal being and the Self of God. God is offered back to God through ideal Human Nature ('To the Father through the features of men's faces').

God, the great Musician, determined all scales—not only the pitches at which he placed selves, but also the essential scapes and types which they assumed, as well as their activities of stress and instress. Pitch established unity by tension; it was the degree of tuning fixed by God on the string of being. Stress, the activity played on the string by God, was grace. All the instress left for the creature to perform was to sigh the wish for correspondence to grace of the marian type (IV. 333).[9] To bring the will to pitch, the soul to stress, was God's work. To keep the will at pitch, to respond by instress, was the creature's work of correspondence inspired by God. To lift the soul from pitch to pitch was also grace. Hopkins arrived at the mystical impasse. In the way of union, how was one to distinguish the acts of self from those of God? 'That is Christ *being me* and me being Christ' (IV. 332). And faith 'is God/in man/knowing his own truth' (IV. 336). Here mystical vision attempted to break through rational limitations. It was not fatalism, even though the self was a mere nothing, a positive infinitesimal in the scale predetermined by God (IV. 331). While the objective world of pitch was relatively infinite—outside the self in possible strains of action—the subjective world was limited to one 'cleave' (exposed face, plane) which the self could see from inside (IV. 328–9).[10] God made use of this limitation, inherent in the self, by exercising his mastery in one dimension (line of direction), in two (area of arc), or in three (elevation in a solid), according to the kind of grace exercised in the will: (1) natural grace, creative act of the Father in the affective will; (2) moral grace, corrective or purifying act of the Son in the elective will; (3) supernatural grace, elevating act of the Spirit, 'God's finger touching the very vein of personality', in the bare self (IV. 337–8). This

71

was the final modification of the moments of stress set forth in the *Deutschland*: creative stress not felt (stanza 1); redemptive stress felt as purgative and afflictive, followed by bare acknowledgement ('I did say yes') and by elevation (stanzas 2 and 3).[11]

In converting his vision to written form in rough notes of a metaphysics, Hopkins faced great difficulties: (1) He had invented new words, 'prepossessed' by years of special history in his mind, and these were a barrier to immediate communication. (2) He was trying to systematize a primitive vision in essence mystical, a vision pointing to a union between God and the soul so intimate that acts of grace and will could often not be rationally distinguished. (3) He relied increasingly upon Pythagorean imagery (geometrical and musical figures) as means of argument. (4) Platonic and Scotist concepts met with the disapproval of his order: the angelic world of possibles, the priority of ideas, the basing of the opposition between nature and self upon the distinction between mind and will in God, the reduction of free will to a mere sigh of aspiration relying entirely upon grace. While St. Thomas had been acquired as the Jesuit philosopher, Jesuit origins in the founder St. Ignatius were closer to the Franciscans, and Hopkins may have tried to recover old ground.[12] Whatever the reason, Hopkins' commentary on the *Exercises* met no encouragement in 1883 at Stonyhurst, in 1884 at Dublin. The disappointment left its mark in *Spelt from Sibyl's Leaves* and the sonnets of the dark night. In January 1883 Hopkins playfully wrote how Scotus showed freedom to be compatible with necessity. A year later he lamented that Scotus' subtlety overshot his interests, so that he was first misquoted, then misunderstood: 'And so I used to read him with delight' (III. 349). Hopkins gave up attempts to transfer his vision into metaphysics, but hoped to apply it in other scholastic and artistic outlets. The 'increase' of the Scotist years was broken. The sacramental intuition, whereby he had greeted Christ in the naturalistic ideal of inscape, was darkened, then fled away: this was the mystery of Christ's

Nature, Pitch, and Will

absence in the dark sonnets. There remained the world of possibles for infinite speculation; the later Greek studies and musical discoveries occupied angelic spheres where Platonic ideas could range freely.

PART IV. BREAKAGE 1884-1889

12. ECHOING MEMORY

In the 1880's, when Hopkins occupied teaching posts at Stonyhurst and Dublin, he hoped to use his scholastic abilities in the service of his vocation by studying and writing for publication. The unfinished commentary on the *Spiritual Exercises* was but the first of many ill-fated plans. When he failed to make his spiritual scheme acceptable, he turned to literary and philosophical scholarship—to Greek verse (study of Homer, Aeschylus, Pindar), language (Greek and Egyptian names; Welsh, Irish, English dialects), criticism (letters; editions and reviews), science (papers on physics, mathematics, metaphysics).[1] Increasingly he felt the failure to complete or accomplish any sizeable work to be of credit to the Society. Tension between genius and vocation was extreme; Hopkins never doubted where his obedience lay. While his earnest attempts were neither realized nor rewarded, while he felt personal and professional failure keenly, his few important discoveries were not lost: they contributed new advances to his art in poetry and in music. It would be unobservant indeed to underestimate his intense melancholia of 1884–5, his more complete renunciation in the last years, and his original scholarship throughout. The impetus behind these scholarly activities was revealed when he wrote in 1885 that he would be occupied one evening, not in attending a political rally, but in 'unsphering the spirit of Plato or something of the sort' (III. 174).

For Hopkins, memory was a storehouse of unconscious material (collective, racial, and spiritual), containing pagan myth as allegory or mirror imagery in a primitive world of 'forepitch' where dwelt the types, examplars, or mothering forms in God's mind prior to actual existence. Man could see, though but darkly, into the glass of universal being, of common nature. There, under all levels, was creation reaching out for Christ. There, God's order of intention echoed with divine harmonies, broken by dissonance, to be resolved upon the keynote of sacrifice. This angelic sphere was like the musical unconscious or spiritual preconscious of Plato, to be distinguished from the automatic or deaf unconscious of Freud.[2] In this primitive world was projected the great Idea of creation and redemption through Christ—an angelic procession to sacrifice in the wilderness outside God, the sacrifice to be the eucharistic Victim for which the Blessed Virgin ministered the matter. The angels joined by covenant in the grand design through music of their heavenly spheres. Lucifer drew rebel angels into a counterpoint of dissonance, until St. Michael in defence of the Virgin led the heavenly hosts against the rebels (IV. 343–351). St. John's apocalyptic vision of the woman with child, attacked by the dragon, and rescued by St. Michael (Revelation xii), was but one of those primitive memories surviving in myth of a mysterious region of God's ideal plan; mythic survivals from other parts of the world testified to the universality of the Christian type scored on the human mind. Basically, the universal myth of creation and redemption reflected the Godhead:

> This sacrifice and this outward procession is a consequence and shadow of the procession of the Trinity, from which mystery sacrifice takes its rise. . . . It is as if the blissful agony or stress of selving in God had forced out drops of sweat or blood, which drops were the world, or as if the lights lit at the festival of that 'peaceful Trinity' through some little cranny striking out lit up into being one 'cleave' out of the world of possible creatures. (IV. 344–5)

In this long note dated 1881 Hopkins systematized his vision, set forth in the *Deutschland* and subsequent poems, of the incarnation as the stem of stress in creation and redemption; and the primacy of Christ was established, with Franciscan and Scotist certainty, in the intentional order 'before all worlds' as well as in the existential order. Even after the commentary on the *Exercises* failed to win acceptance, Hopkins continued to search ancient customs and texts to support his vision of the great Idea.

Elements of the mythic vision (procession, sacrifice, battle, songs of creation and redemption) along with angelic personages (angels and devils, woman and child, dragon and champion) were partially recoverable from pagan legends. The relationship of the shadow to the true type, of pagan image to Christian exemplar, fascinated Hopkins: hence his interest in the archetypal Corpus Christi procession, in primitive methods of sacrifice, in angelic theophanies of Christ, in dragons (1. 149, 161; II.102). Homeric studies led him in 1886 to investigate the Egyptian prototypes of Greek deities and to find among them a trinity of gods and a tradition of sacrifice (III. 260, 278), showing anticipations of the Trinity and of Christ's passion. In Hopkins' time anthropological studies of rituals and religions were beginning; Frazer's *Golden Bough* was to be first published in 1890. Yet, clearly differentiating between dark human mirrors and the light of revelation, Hopkins looked with horror upon the untruth of Greek mythology, and claimed it could only be redeemed by allegorical treatment (II. 146–147).

The allegory of woman and dragon entered two of Hopkins' sonnets: *Andromeda* (No. 49), a public sonnet on the political situation of the Church; *Spelt from Sibyl's Leaves* (No. 62), a private sonnet on judgement. In the first, 'Time's Andromeda' was the Roman Church militant in England ('on this rock rude'), persecuted in the past, now threatened from the West by industrial mob-rule ('A wilder beast'). The lawless beast was worse than others. Who was to save the Church in England? Perseus—that is, the Church's champion, St. Michael the Archangel.[3] Perseus would free Andromeda from 'thongs' of death with sword, from 'fangs' of dragon sin 'With Gorgon's gear'. The later sonnet, *Sibyl's Leaves*, interpreted a cosmological vision of heaven and earth as a sign of the last things.[4] Here was an inversion of the Christian story of woman and dragon, for 'boughs dragonish' were in the grotto of the heart, while in the sky was a mock-image of the Virgin, evening, straining to become the mother of all being. Evening was but a part of the vision of good and evil which was interpreted or 'spelt' allegorically as a warning of death and judgement upon the soul.

While Andromeda and Sibyl were taken from old sources, there were two companion-sonnets of 1887 based on more immediate materials, also for purposes of allegory, both public sonnets on the British worker. *Tom's Garland* (No. 66), warning of discontent in the commonweal, projected the body politic as one man from head (gold crown of sovereign) to foot (hobnail boots of daylabourer), a body threatened by wolfpacks (outcasts from the commonweal). *Harry Ploughman* (No. 67), celebrating obedience in physical work, pictured the labourer as he should be: a body like a ship steered by the grey eye of wisdom,[5] with many members working together like a ship's crew called at a roll-call to stand ready, then lean together in co-ordination of 'sinew-service'. The alternation of stress and slack in Harry's muscular fibres (an embodiment of will at pitch) was brought out by juxtapositions: 'fall to; | Stand at stress' and 'sucked or sank— | Soared or sank'. In the act of ploughing up furrows of earth, Harry was a ship ploughing the sea and casting up spray. The activity of dedicated service exploded with flames of sacrificial glory. Metaphorical extension of the ploughman as a ship, Piers Plowman in naval terms, meant that this Harry was in himself an ideal commonweal in action, baroque emblem of militant service. In these two complex sonnets Hopkins allegorized the current gospel of work (set forth by Carlyle and Ruskin) in the Christian tradition of St. Paul and St. Augustine.

Now allegory, based on levels of correspondence—natural and moral, pagan and Christian—was implicit in much of Hopkins' work as a source of metaphor, even though it could not be full-fledged allegory without a narrative framework (such as the two wreck-poems, each with a ship of souls wrecked, involving issues of providence and salvation). Hopkins used analogy constantly. When analogy included personification

or impersonation he had implicit allegory: 'Hope holds to
Christ the mind's own mirror out' (No. 113): 'What is . . .
delightful dene? | Wedlock. What is water? Spousal love' (No.
121). When analogy became a pair of mirroring levels, they
were resonant with exchanged sound, musical echoes. Two
strains of thought were discovered by Hopkins in the Greek
choruses: the underthought was 'an echo or shadow of the
overthought, something like canons and repetitions in music',
although sometimes the underthought might be independent
(III. 253).

That reflexion or echo usually meant more than the Platonic
dualism of idea-image has already been found in Hopkins' conception of verse as inscape of spoken sound, 'speech wholly or
partially repeating the same figure of sound' (IV. 249). Verse
inscape had given him the principle of diatonic beauty as
chime, 'brilliancy, starriness, quain, margaretting' (IV. 251).
Now chime in sound-inscape was linked to inner oneness, pitch,
and pitch of being gave chime of doing as identifying echo of
self: 'Deals out that being indoors each one dwells; | Selves—
goes itself; *myself* it speaks and spells' (No. 57). Although the
secret self could not be known, its outer echoes could be. These
echoes were mounted as 'sakes' on the specific type or species to
which the individual belonged. Sake was the distinctive mark a
being had outside itself—not merely echo, reflexion, shadow,
name—but the distinctive quality in the mark, clearness, light,
bulk, genius, for sake was the echo tuned to one pitch that
could deal out inward being.[6] Henry Purcell (No. 45) could be
identified by 'quaint moonmarks', the crescent-shaped inci-
dentals (mordents, trills, and other turns) bound into his inscape of the species, 'the make of man' (melodic curvature).[7]
Corresponding to sakes of the individual there were 'keepings'
of specific poetic schools. Keepings, as part of nature, could
be replaced with but little loss—as dialect, a west-country
keeping, in Barnes—or as native properties in American and
English verse exchanged through a ' "ciphering" note on an
organ' (I. 83, 87–8, 192; II. 98–9). While every art school was
a species with keepings, every true or original artist was like

a species in nature with individually distinctive qualities
(III. 370).

Echo revealed inner being; myth pointed to Christian type;
everything in nature rightly perceived contained inscapes
which held a world of ideas. Even physical science could lead
to basic metaphysical principles, for mechanics contained what
was beyond mechanics. The true hexagonal section of honey-
comb had mechanical symmetry; once grant the honeybee a
special instinct for shaping cells in that way, then one passed
beyond mechanical necessity to an inner instinct 'like the
specific songs of cuckoo and thrush' (I. 281). Scape became
inscape, and inscape determined specific being. From a primitive underworld of instinct, the angelic notes of divine harmonies could be heard, rung clear to the visionary senses, or
seen in a fairyland of the blue ideal, of light, stars, angels:

Rafts and rafts of flake-leaves light, dealt so, painted on the air,
Hang as still as hawk or hawkmoth, as the stars or as the angels
    there,
Like the thing that never knew the earth, never off roots
Rose. (No. 121)

Going beyond the Pre-Raphaelite vision of creation as a paradise, Hopkins saw the hypostatic order, the angelic or pre-
human region, where types were lodged or locked into ideas.
Here Christ was 'steaded' in angelic theophanies of the Old
Testament. Here creation bore the prepossession of the incarnation and the pagan world of nature bore the impress of the
Christian design of grace.

All the world of ideal types was potentially recoverable from
the underthought of mind, mythic and preconscious memory, a
territory of mysteries bearing the great Idea of creation and redemption. Memory, image of being, source of intellect and will,
was the deep well through which infused grace sustained nature
in the ground of being. Memory training kept the will in order,
the mirrors clear; and memory training was practised by Hopkins. Along with many other Jesuits in the 1880's, Hopkins
learned and exercised Loisette's system (III. 425, 451).[8] Professor Alphonse Loisette (Marcus Dwight Larrowe) lectured on

physiological memory as an assimilative power, a making of the intellect 'stay' (Hopkins' 'hold', 'fasten', 'stall') with the senses in order that vast stores of information could be readily memorized: the method was one of immediate identification through association, translating from one sense to another, or from number to letter. The mneumonics involved numbers, treating numbers as words. And numbers were for Hopkins mentally interesting, for he contributed remarks on a visionary field of numbers to his father's *The Cardinal Numbers* (1887) (I. 321–2). It was through numbers and mathematics that he hoped to strengthen his metaphysics and incidentally his art.

13. NUMBER, METRE, AND MUSIC

WHILE Hopkins' investigations of mythic memory took him more deeply into the realm of ideal essence, he wished for a science whereby he could prove his insight. He speculated about the mathematical basis of art, hoping thereby to enter the field of metaphysics and arrive at a general philosophy. Beginning with mathematical proportion in art, he groped from proportion to ratio and from laws of ratio to counterpoint. Mathematics eventually advanced both his metrics and his music. He shared this interest with George Herbert.[1]

Hopkins' favourite verse forms, dithyrambic ode and Italian sonnet, had mathematical proportions based on the simple ratios of 1 : 2 (approximately) and 4 : 3. He never tired of the sonnet structure. In the cipher 14 there was no mystery, but in the strict sonnet of octave and sestet there was the ideal equation '$(4 + 4) + (3 + 3) = 2.4 + 2.3 = 2(4 + 3) = 2.7 = 14$': this structure corresponded to the division of metres by caesura (division of hexameter and ionic trimeter, cited by St. Augustine), giving the Pythagorean equation $3^2 + 4^2 = 5^2$, and also corresponded to musical scales and modes (pentachord + tetrachord) (II. 71–2). Sonnet ratios thus had a clear relation to ratios in metre and in music.

Hopkins noted that musical and metrical time, arising from the dance, went by twos and fours, establishing a mental frame of fours, symmetry or quadrature; this frame was a limit, so that in a verse line three feet could be expanded to four with pleasure, but four feet could not be added to (I. 119–120). The naturalistic ideal for metre was then a frame of fours (scape) with a beat of threes (stress), a ratio of 4 : 3 (inscape).[2] When Hopkins developed his verse forms he maintained proportion (the sonnet of 4 + 4 + 3 + 3) and when he elaborated form within the verse line he discovered counterpoint (the sprung Alexandrine of 4/3 + 4/3). Not in music but in metre Hopkins first found the nature of counterpoint; through the

Alexandrine he developed a counterpoint of fixed ratios. The Alexandrine was divided by caesura into 3 + 3. Hopkins treated it as two half-lines, each with a mental frame of fours: it became dimeter, two bars of four feet each, with one foot silent at the pause in each bar (a stress of 3 in a scape of 4, or 4/3 + 4/3). When he adapted the Alexandrine to blank verse in tragedy, he allowed more variety, either expanding 3 to 4 or suppressing 4 to 3 stresses, adapting the measure to dramatic changes (III. 360).

When Hopkins began serious work on Greek metres in 1886, he believed he had discovered in the asymmetrical ratio of 4 : 3 the true scansion of half of Greek and Latin lyric verse. The Dorian measure had originally been 'a march step in three-time executed in four steps to the bar', which had developed by resolving one crotchet of three (— — —) and never the last; irregularities and licences appeared: 'Out of this simple combination of numbers, three and four, . . . arose the structure of most of Pindar's odes and most of the choral odes in the drama' (I. 233). The principle extended from metre to music: the octave and the old heptachord scales both arose from doubled tetrachords, overlapping in one case, free in the other (I. 235).

For Hopkins there was profound truth in these number combinations. Why did he maintain they were founded deeply in nature? To understand this, it is necessary to understand the interworking of numbers in Pythagorean theory (evident in Plato and traced in Christian allegorists like St. Augustine).[3] The Pythagorean doctrine of numbers took as the beginning of all figures and qualities the right-angled triangle, consisting of the numbers 3, 4, 5, in the equation $3^2 + 4^2 = 5^2$. Three stood for the heavenly triangle, four for the earth-square. The sum of the first three numbers, the triad, was the number of the whole, a unity in multiplicity, cause of all things; the sum of the first four numbers, the tetractys or quadrate, was the root of eternally flowing nature. If the numeral system were treated as a scale of fixed points and intervals, number was found to be the source of rhythm (metre) and harmonia (music). Fixed points expressed the limiting (finite nature) and intermediate spaces the unlimited (infinite supernature). Extension came about by the intervention of infinite in finite or three into four. For instance, geometrical extension in three dimensions was based on a threefold interval between four points. The infinite was breathed into the finite, contraries bound together, and harmonies born: all relations could be brought to a standard in the musical octave or heptachord whereby number and harmony became the source of all truth. Plato added to the Pythagorean theory the doctrine that the objects of mathematical science, numbers, were intermediate between the sensibles and the ideas, so that he attempted to deduce a philosophy of ideas from sensibles through mathematics.[4]

Hopkins' fascination for numbers, fixed points in a scale, made his Platonic Realism thoroughly Pythagorean. He was following St. Augustine and Plato in using numbers derived from sense-objects as symbols of ideas. In metre and music he was groping from physical sounds through mathematics to metaphysical origins, from matter through number to spirit. He began to study mathematics more intently in 1887, regaining an old hope to build a philosophy of art on science, and perhaps, having established himself firmly in philosophy, to be able to generalize in other fields. While writing out his paper on Dorian to be read before a club at University College, Dublin, he believed he could establish 'metre and music . . . on a scientific footing . . . final like the law of gravitation' (III. 377). Soon he was trying to ground his metrical theory in metaphysics by subjecting geometrical terms to analysis and he was inventing new words for his philosophy (III. 379).[5] A technique based on counterpointed numbers (the ratio of 4 : 3 expressing the right-angled triangle and the right angle related to 'quain')[6] was fruitful in Hopkins' verse and music. But was he extending his insight into metaphysics in order to formulate the interweaving of nature and grace on a basis of numerical combinations (earth numbers being even, heaven numbers odd)? The surviving manuscript material does not tell us.

Now numbers had fulfilment in combinations on a scale of

84

measured notes and intervals, in music. As verse became increasingly laborious for Hopkins, he began to compose music, finding in melodic numbers a readier inspiration (I. 136).[7] All his music was written for voice, at first with external accompaniment, much later with integral counterpoint. He began composing under great handicaps: he had a delicate ear, a fine singing voice, but no formal training on musical instruments. He took up violin, then piano, but found reading difficult. Yet with Platonic confidence he composed from melodic ideas downwards to the instrument: 'all keys are the same to me and to every one who thinks that music was before instruments and angels before tortoises and cats' (I. 289–90). While he found his friends' poems songful, flying into tunes, he could not set his own airs and frequently called on his sister Grace for assistance, until in 1880 he took up theory of harmony in earnest (I. 103, 105–6, 112). He could not master the modern harmony of vertical chords, so different from the older Greek harmony of horizontal melody. Increasingly he was driven to experiment by constructing counterpoint to his own linear melodies; by 1883 he was earnestly submitting compositions to musical authorities for correction,[8] but still wavering between modern harmony and counterpoint (I. 125–6, 136, 153, 173, 178, 182): 'I fumble a little at music, at counterpoint. . . . If I could get to accompany my own airs I should, so to say, enter into a new kingdom at once, for I have plenty of tunes ready' (II. 109). In the face of great difficulties in reading and playing, Hopkins was discovering inscape of pitched sound for himself. At first he satisfied himself with a single melody in a homely minor key, following the native British range of twelve notes within which to rise, fall, turn, repeat, suspend, resolve—in tunes set to the nature verse of Bridges (the *Spring Odes*) and Dixon (*Fallen Rain*), where melody was a line of feeling noted with stresses. He admired splendid octave falls, cross-rhythms, quarter-tones (III. 331; II. 169–70). He combined triplets with couplets in counterpoint of 3 : 2 and tried to apply a double system of both octave and heptachord scales (I. 208, 234–5).

Once he began studying harmony, a new kingdom slowly unfolded. True to the distinctive underlining in Purcell's works, Hopkins introduced into music to the *Battle of the Baltic* 'a long ground bass, a chime of fourteen notes, repeated ten times running, with the treble moving freely above it', and thought the effect would orchestrate well for bells (I. 201–2, 207–8). Clearly for Hopkins, harmony was being treated as counterpoint. On the verge of musical discovery his pieces made 'a new departure and more like volcanic sunsets or sunrises in the musical hemisphere than anythin ye can conçave' (I. 202). Counterpoint was to help Hopkins pass from music of bare feeling to music of higher power—against Germanic mood music back to the masculine airs of Old England, 'the bone, frame, and *charpente*' (I. 180). Relying on counterpoint in the diatonic keyboard, he rejected modulation in favour of the primitive modes of plainchant and ancient music. In doing so he faced not only the doubts of Bridges, but those of accomplished musicians he consulted, for they found his music dated from before the piano and was written for another keyboard. Hopkins' return to the primitive system was deliberate; to his ear modern harmony was crude; plainchant in the older authentic and plagal modes was rich by simplicity (I. 213–14, 219–20).

He was conscious of trying to achieve a rhetorical technique in music, based on a world of profound mathematics. When music came in lines of harmony, it was 'bound up . . . with the tune of the principal part' (II. 135–6). The underparts became echoes of the melody, then independent in form and phrasing. Increasingly the piano became a drawback: Hopkins conceived his tunes vocally and interwove them mentally. In reaching for a peculiar English dissonance, sounding major and minor chords from the same root, he was following in the tradition of Blow and Purcell. Finally in 1888, contrapuntalism became his established principle. He found that his authentic airs took to fugue and canon quite easily; they could be woven or 'margaretted' in question and answer at an octave or a third higher or lower every two or four bars. When his exacting teacher, Sir Robert Stewart, finally approved his counterpoint exercise on Patmore's *Crocus*, he began to inherit his kingdom:

Success in canon beats the other successes of art: it comes like a miracle, even to the inventor. It does seem as if the canon discovered the musician and not he it. But the truth is that in a really organic tune the second or third strain or both tend to be good counterpoint (with or even without bass) to the first. And then fugue is really canon at the fifth (or twelfth). So that I see a world of canon and fugue before me. I do not say I am going there. But one madrigal in canon I will finish and then I hope one in fugue. No accompaniments; and the human voice is immortal. You said nothing would come: I hope you may have been wrong. (I. 278)

Up until his death Hopkins continued to work in canon. His last modification was to treat the air as a generic form freshly specified in strict canon for each verse of a poem (I. 305). The madrigal skein, closely interwoven, eliminated the disproportion between air and setting. The air governing its echoes rang out with its 'doing-be', for integral counterpoint revealed rather than obscured melodic being.

14. THE COMBAT

HOPKINS as a Jesuit was bound in loyalty to an army of the Church militant. He was a soldier of Christ. He saw in outward military service, in garb and conduct of men of duty and war, signs of an imitation of Christ. So in the sonnet *The Soldier* (No. 63), the knight of Christ-like deed was greeted by Christ himself.[1] But inward service in the spiritual combat was harder yet. Hopkins' combat came through spiritual desolation in 1884–5. There were manifold outward symptoms, physical, emotional, and intellectual, while within there was darkness and tumult of soul.[2] Hopkins interpreted the warfare as a battle of the lone will from which natural consolation and even grace itself had been torn. The sense of frustration through failure to complete scholastic projects was intensified by a feeling of exile in his teaching post in Ireland and extended to a nervous depression. Hopkins confronted a winter world of barren prayer and barren work in an alien land. His heart began a long night watch against a panorama of last things. The experience entered 'unbidden' into verse (I. 221); thereby he objectified the combat, estimated the spiritual forces involved, and could exert intellectual control at least over the soul's suffering. The agony of desolation and despair began in *Spelt from Sibyl's Leaves* (No. 62) and in Caradoc's soliloquy (No. 105, Act II), until with all externals removed the loneliness of bare self, pitch, or soul, became the battleground for the sonnets of holy terror.

The dark-night series of six sonnets (Nos. 64, 65, 68, 69, 70, 71), difficult to arrange in chronological order, constituted an inner dialogue between head and heart, turning over the issues of comfort and torment, uttering prayers by question, statement, ejaculation. The condensed syntax, marked by interjections, negatives, inversions, represented spiritual stress and slack upon the strands of selfbeing, while turns of thought were moulded to units of quatrain and tercet within the sonnet

88

structure. After the vigil had developed into an intense inner struggle, Hopkins reached a point where he could look back over the situation with ironic detachment. In *Carrion Comfort* (No. 64) he was both protagonist wrestling with an angelic incubus or bestial nightmare and spectator at the match wondering doubtfully—'since (seems) I kissed the rod, hand rather'—whom to cheer, his Antagonist or his soul, the Victor or the victim? And which was which? Who really had won? By shift in tense from present to past, the sestet embraced the entire action of the series. The fight was over: 'That night, that year | Of now done darkness'. Uncertain joy emerged from the still ambiguous war. He had obeyed, could scarcely believe he had been miserable enough to fight against 'God's will be done', saw in a delayed flash the truth: 'I wretch lay wrestling with (my God!) my God.' The other sonnets remained in the immediate action of the present, but self-accusation continued ('Wretch').

'No worst' (No. 65) set forth a paradox of comfort in the school of prayer. The soul facing the sense of abandonment suffered agony: 'My God, my God, why hast thou forsaken me?' Christ had departed. Only the elements of the annunciation were left to pray to: the Holy Ghost the Comforter and Mary the mother of mercy. Where were comfort and relief to be found? Pangs of prayer, well-schooled in self-torment, increased in pain and ferocity, a main sorrow as wild as ocean main (pivoting on the word) battering cliffs on the anvil of the world, the hard world of grief on grief. Hopkins recognized his earlier comfort (a sacramental naturalism in poems of 1876-7) as 'cheap | May' compared to the inner trial, the vertical of the spirit.[3] He became ironic schoolmaster to his own heart: comfort or counterpane on bed supplied the only comfort available, sleep the only relief, in the absence of spiritual comforts. The tumult subsiding fell into a deep gap of separation—from family, country, heaven and hell in 'To seem' (No. 68); from God in 'I wake' (No. 69). Here (No. 68) the paradox of Christ, 'he my peace my parting', went home to the soul, cut off by religion from family and country, now fallen among Irish political confusions of war, 'at a third remove'. Each 'remove' was a removal from creative resources, from the roots of consolation; hence the underthought of courtship ('woos'), marriage ('wife'), and birth ('breeds'). Heaven and hell both conspired against the 'wisest word' or best efforts of prayer and work. Then Christ, having isolated the soul, himself left it desolate (No. 69). In the darkness of dry prayer without God, in the delay of his light, the soul arrived at the frightening paradox of condemnation: if God did not reply to the soul's letters of prayer, attempts at correspondence to grace, then 'cries like dead letters' fell back upon the self and God had cursed the soul to taste how bitter it was without him, a foretaste of damnation as removal from God.[4]

Recovery came through forced acts of patience and charity in the dry will. *Patience* (No. 70) set forth its paradox: patience involved wounds and the healing of wounds.[5] Patience meant war, the spiritual combat of the passion, renunciation to the wounds and the weariness through mortification, chastisement, obedience. Without these things the healing power of patience—an ivy vine of heart-shaped leaves covering ruins—could not root and work. The poet now turned from the third person of detached speech (in the octave) to the 'we' and 'our' of Christ's warfaring company (in the sestet): 'our hearts', 'rebellious wills', had to be coerced to particular obedience, to acts of utter resignation: 'Into thy hands I commend my spirit' in everything. Christ, himself waiting patiently in the holy tabernacle (a beehive), could distil grace through eucharistic wafers ('His crisp combs', honeycombs). In the last sonnet of the series, 'My own heart' (No. 71), there was a final paradox of trust and doubt in self-charity. The soul was called to relaxation, in trust that God would return in his own way and time. The protagonist, leaving the prison of self-involved self-torment and addressing his 'poor Jackself' with tragi-comic common sense, shrugged sceptically at comfort: 'let joy size [seize; grow] | At God knows when to God knows what'. He regained holy humour in a counsel of wit. Comfort could

not come from the barren efforts of self, but only from the unex-
pected graces of God—from the heaven-in-earth of Christ's
two natures, 'as skies | Betweenpie mountains'. Recovery was
managed through a measure of self-detachment, and the dialogue ending in equivocation was thus linked back to the
sestet of *Carrion Comfort.*

The struggle was a purgation (separating grain from chaff,
No. 64), extending over a lifetime ('I mean years, mean life',
No. 69), and striking universal experience ('world-sorrow', No.
65). It was a purgation not of the senses but of the soul, the
dark night of the soul in the mystical way. By taking issue
with himself in more than one voice, the poet set up an objective point of view to play upon a series of mystical para-
doxes: the impasse in distinguishing who was the hero of the
combat, God or soul, so close was the wrestling union of Victor
and victim (No. 64); the impassable path between gorge and
precipice, with the escape into comfort of bed (No. 65); the
isolation in union with Christ, together with the strange baffle-
ment of sterility in which heaven and earth were working at
once, both good and evil (No. 68); the proximity of the purgation from self to the sense of utter damnation (No. 69); the
duality of patience, warlike wounds and peaceful healing (No.
70); the inversion of self-pity into ironic detachment from the
comfort desired (No. 71).

Themes of time, night, war, obedience, surrender in the
other poems of Hopkins' last years came out of the main combat. Often he would objectify the problems of spiritual discipline outside himself in human mirrors. He knew that, while
earth of its nature gazed and groped towards heaven (No. 111),
men had to brace moral will to the divine by military obedience. Such were the imperatives of command: in the march of
beauty, 'gaze out of countenance' from nature to grace (No.
61); in the soldier, 'Mark Christ our King', the true warrior
(No. 63); in the ploughman, notice the sinew-service in action.
'Harry bends, look' (No. 67). Tom, Dick, and Harry, as well as
'Jack-self' Hopkins, were to be changed into something else—
not merely to become better co-ordinated individuals or better

members of a commonweal—but to become Christ, the perfect Manhood, immortal diamond. What was the price? It was martyrdom, the key of sacrifice in the passion.

Man could be a worthy or an unworthy combatant, high or low, to be eulogized or satirized. In *St. Alphonsus Rodriguez* (No. 73) Hopkins celebrated a Jesuit lay brother whose secret conquest of evil spirits won him recognition as a saint. Here the poet acknowledged two kinds of heroic martyrdom: the external combat with physical marks of war and the echo of fame ('Honour is flashed off exploit'), and 'the war within' without outward manifestation ('Earth hears no hurtle then from fiercest fray'). These corresponded to God's two stresses or shaping powers set forth in the sestet: the outer hewing of creative grace and the inner growth of redemptive or sacramental grace. However, human pretensions to heroism were easily satirized: so in 'The shepherd's brow' (No. 122), 'Man Jack the man is, just; his mate a hussy'. The mould of man was no lightning forehead of shepherd, no high tower of angel, but a 'scaffold of score brittle bones', brief in breath. A human skeleton was no instrument for tragedy. One could see mortality, the death's head, by looking at spoon reflexions. The human conflict was but a storm in a teacup. The low view of man was best maintained in scornful quibbles—'He!', 'bass' (base), 'viol' (vile), 'masque' (mask). Such were two possibilities for man—the high or the low, sanctity or mediocrity, the heroic warrior or the mere Jack, the immortal soul or the mortal flesh. Between these two, man swayed in a lifetime. He had to lean, by bias of pitch, one way or the other in the race of life. The pitch of will preoccupied the poet in his elegy on lost youth, *On the Portrait of Two Beautiful Young People* (No. 119). The subjects, the Archbold children, were noticeably older than the portrait when Hopkins saw them ('dark tramplers, tyrant years'). In the portrait, the girl leaning, the boy looking beyond, the brother and sister were a forelock of time, a cluster of natural virtues, ripe for the opportunity of good or evil, swaying in the scales of choice. Where was their guide, 'landmark, seamark, or soul's star', in the voyage of life? The poet

directed their ship of souls to Christ as truth and wondered
about their secret pitch, the 'list' of the ship:

> Man lives that list, that leaning in the will
> No wisdom can forecast by gauge or guess,
> The selfless self of self, most strange, most still,
> Fast furled and all foredrawn to No or Yes.

Leaning meant pitch or direction of will, 'foredrawn' in the
dark mirror of mysterious destiny, yet not 'forecast' in the
clear view of knowledge. It was a precarious and secret thing,
a free unknown. Imagery of weight and measures conveyed the
main thought of decision hanging in the balance of the free will.

Among stern moral counsels, the hymn 'Thee, God, I come
from, to thee go' (No. 116) signified the gentler sway of God's
hand, controlling the priest at the altar as the source controls
the fountain. The priest, surrendering in penitence to sacramental stress of mercy, then turned mercy towards his brother,
'Man my mate and counterpart'. On terms of such intimacy
with his Lord, Hopkins could 'contend' quietly with God, not
in combat, but in case at law, laying forth in direct address
('sir') his dryness against the world's plenteous renewal, and
asking very simply for grace to build some work: 'send my
roots rain' (No. 74). Finally Hopkins gave his artistic last
testament to Bridges, *To R. B.* (No. 75). He admitted the
time-gap between inspiration and the finished art-work in a
little myth: inspiration was breath ('spur', both spirit and
urgency) to which fire in the mind answered, as a current of
air gave flame in a blowpipe; so fertilized by insight the mind
stored away the embryonic work as a woman carried a child,
while the work was being perfected through acquired rhetoric.
Hopkins needed, relied upon, the Holy Spirit as his inspiration,
'the sire of muse', and without such infused grace from his
Apollo or Christ his poetry lacked the joy and song of creation.
So Hopkins confessed the relation of prayer to poetry and of
change in prayer to change in poetry.

The most complete objectification and most successful reso-
lution of the spiritual warfare came in a long sonnet of sprung
Alexandrines and three codas, *That Nature is a Heraclitean*

Fire and of the comfort of the Resurrection (No. 72). Here the combat became the battle of the elements in storm around the central fire of nature (from Heraclitus and early Greek thought). Pagan pessimism in the mortal flux of nature and man confronted, and was reversed by, Christian optimism in the resurrection of the body. That was the general content. But the particular arrangement came from Augustinian and Franciscan exemplarism: creaturely types showing forth the Creator in the scale or ladder of creation.[6] According to the Franciscan St. Bonaventure there were three grades of created existence imitating the divine Essence and only completed by Christ himself as Archetype: (1) *umbra*/shadow (the elements), (2) *vestigium*/footprint (the animals), (3) *imago*/reflexion (the souls and spirits), and finally (4) *lumen*/light (God).[7] Hopkins following this scheme (more systematic than that employed in No. 57) set forth: (1) shadow in stormclouds (marching and fighting as an army of air and water),[8] (2) footprint in mud-creases (marks left by wind wrestling with earth), (3) reflexion in man's mental sparks (thrown off from fire), (4) light shining from the cross in glory (a sea-beacon to the ship of the soul).[9] Key words traced out this fourfold procession: (1) 'shivelights and shadow-tackle', (2) 'Squadroned masks and manmarks . . . | Footfretted', (3) 'her clearest-selvèd spark | . . . firedint', (4) 'an eternal beam'. The happy activities of flux in lower nature passed into the tragic extinction of 'mark on mind'. In ascending the scale, creatures mounted from remote and unstable signs to increasingly fixed and distinctive marks, reaching human inscape in 'manshape'. Even man, creation's highest type, was swallowed up in space-time. Then the resurrection arrived, both clarion (*verbum*/Word) and beacon (*lumen de lumine*/Light of Light)—Christ, the eternally fixed Archetype of types. The member in Christ became Christ—*Christus, alter Christus*—changed from glory to glory in the divine equation 'immortal diamond, | Is immortal diamond'. The Jack of mere earth, carbonaceous body in mortality, was at once transformed into sacred substance fit for heaven, resurrection body in glory, and so was crystallized into eternity.

15. CONCLUSION

In both art and religion Hopkins was closely linked with his times. The Oxford movement of Pusey and Newman overtook him in his pursuit of classical studies: he became first an Anglo-Catholic, then a Roman Catholic and a Jesuit. The Pre-Raphaelite movement of painters and poets, together with the critics Ruskin and Pater, gave him his artistic context: he became painter, poet, and critic too. Then, while the debate between science and religion was going on, Hopkins developed a theory of art using the best of both worlds—the laws of science and the life of religion—combining wild naturalism (type of Mary) with religious idealism (type of Christ). On the one hand, there was a Romantic return to primitive innocence of sensations; on the other, a Christian striving towards the perfect Manhood. Here was the peculiar Pre-Raphaelite tension between angelic heaven and fleshly earth, without any of its sickliness, for Hopkins' work was free from two Victorian diseases—subjective dream indulgence in vogues of escape and reverie, brooding exploitation of confused emotionalism and passive sensationalism. In Hopkins all had the immediacy and 'rash-fresh' clarity of authentic vision, the intensity of honest sensations and emotions.

The problem of the Victorian age was its divorce of ideal theory and practical vision, together with the substitution of ethical for religious and metaphysical values. In verse there was a double weakening: the blight of archaic diction (often pseudo-Elizabethan) and the effeminacy of exotic forms (French verse forms of the rondeliers). The triumph of Hopkins' achievement was a heightening of living language, a reinforcement of familiar forms by native stress, an illuminative integration of vision and theory, an exhilarating conquest of religious meaning, by which even failure (in the dark sonnets) was made victorious. Behind the vision of nature, under the wilderness and sufferings of the world,

Hopkins discovered no dry theory but a lively one, echoing with the songs of creation and redemption. Nature rang with sympathetic analogies.[1] As in George Herbert, all nature was seen in terms of a musical metaphor, and there was ultimate harmony, harmony of nature in grace where innocence and perfection were to be restored after the universal extension of sacrifice.

Beyond his fellow Victorians Hopkins was faithful to his poetic voice, sometimes denying it utterance, but never forcing it for the sake of mere writing, always relying upon genuine inspiration, always advancing in rhetorical technique. His lack of a reading public was an unforeseen advantage. Many other poets, writing on a par with prose writers, betrayed voice and vision to a mass audience, so that at the core of their works are found hesitancy and evaporation of meaning. The problem of private vision assuming public voice and aimed at a large, undefined audience made the longer works of Tennyson and Browning tedious (*Idylls*, the *Ring*) and actually put an end to the poet in Arnold.[2] The problem of Hopkins was the reverse: public vision of creation and redemption revealed by private oracle and received by a very few, the audience widening only long after the death of the poet.

Placing Hopkins' poetry in the English poetic tradition has been found a difficult task. Various schools have been invoked along with his name—Wordsworthian, Miltonic, Keatsian or Pre-Raphaelite, the alliterative school of Middle English, the new metaphysical school of Patmore and Thompson. Each of these influenced Hopkins at some stage in his development; the Pre-Raphaelite school was the most significant. If a distinct label is needed, perhaps 'baroque' is almost satisfactory, expressing the vehement and fiery incarnation of idea in word-made-flesh, the word rendered sensational. Jesuit tradition in the baroque style links Hopkins directly to the seventeenth-century poetic experience of controlled violence and surprise, of Christian feeling infusing and commanding classical forms, and thus he recalls the poetry of Donne, Herbert, Crashaw, Quarles, and Benlowes.[3] Yet how did this happen in the nineteenth century? It must not be forgotten that Pre-Raphaelite art arranged realistic detail of nature for ideal message-value, to tell a story or embody an idea, and that this technique carried on, in a new key, the old tradition of the baroque emblem-books. The verse-picture combination of the black and white emblem came to coloured life in the poetry-painting association of Pre-Raphaelite art: not only were pictures painted to illustrate poems and vice versa, but book-illustration in art and word-painting in literature were widely popular. In Hopkins Pre-Raphaelite symbolism and Jesuit emblem-tradition met in a new baroque, independent and fresh, for Hopkins remained deliberately his own species, unique, as he thought all poets should be (III. 370).

Hopkins' three great technical advances were in diction, rhythm, and texture. For him poetic diction meant 'current language heightened'. He sought out provincialisms and coinages native to the concrete and living roots of language, combining these specific marks into alogical, co-ordinated, and exclamatory periods. Sprung rhythm derived force and flow, not from haphazard accents, but from high stresses important to 'fetch out' the sense by emphasis. The style was declamatory, interpretative, and followed a free pattern fitting the individual phrase or line of thought—reminiscent of Purcell's bold liberties and surprises threaded on a continuous melodic line. But the new metre and the new language would have been frigid innovations without the entire expressional texture fused with them—chiming of consonants and alliteration of vowels—a concatenation of syllables similar to Welsh systems of lettering. Neglect of this rich overlay of textural echo would result in a loss, not of a mere ornament, but of the very nature of sprung rhythm.

Along with advances in language and rhetorical technique, Hopkins left to the poetic tradition significant contributions in lyric form, especially in sonnet and ode. Concentrating on the Petrarchan sonnet, with its careful balance of octave and sestet, Hopkins experimented in contracted and expanded modes (curtal sonnets Nos. 37, 46, 111; Alexandrine sonnets outriding Nos. 45, 53, 61, 63, 64; caudated sonnets Nos. 66, 67, 72), always maintaining basic rhymes and proportions 2(4) + 2(3). Expanded sonnets were the more important, in order to make the English sonnet equal in length to the Italian (II. 85–7). Lines were lengthened by extra stresses (to six or eight feet), by extrametrical syllables (outrides), or by additional half-lines (codas and burden-lines); sometimes all three methods were used (No. 72). In each case Hopkins gave his sonnet the orchestral fullness and impact of an ode. He turned to the ode proper in either of two modes—the Horatian or the Pindaric—often with an elegiac intent in view. For the Horatian ode he kept to a series of quatrains written in compressed style of simple tetrameter and/or trimeter (Nos. 24, 128, 129, 41, 110, 116). For the Pindaric he maintained a strophic or stanzaic manner in elaborate metric, frequently dividing the ode into two parts (Nos. 28, 43, 59, 121 incomplete).

Beyond technical advances in versification and contributions in lyric form, Hopkins' poetry wrestled with a strong core of thought (Christian ideas infused with Gothic feeling into classical forms). The three notes of his nature verse—joy, pity, and fear—came to him from his religious life: the joy of creative light in sacramental sonnets of nature, the pity of the compassionate cloud in poems of the pastoral care for men, and the fear of redemptive night in the dark sonnets of personal desolation. Over these notes—the exaltation of joy, the catharsis of pity and fear towards a new joy—was woven his characteristic spiritual imagery: images of the soul as angelic voice or bird (winged *eros* or *psyche*), with its activities of affection as love-lace (organic growth, binding *philia*) and of election as battle-armour (military combat, sacrificial *agape*), based on the mystery of the self (naval or racing course of pitch). Under the poetry there lay the foundations of a life truly lived in honesty with acceptance.

This study has traced the shaping vision of Hopkins (his vision of creation in creative development) from naturalistic idealism through a philosophy of inscape and instress to a

Scotist voluntarism and a Pythagorean Platonism of music, memory, and number. Under the pressure of Greek and Pre-Raphaelite studies, Hopkins' concrete vision soon acquired an abstract theory. Vision and theory interlocked in his pursuit of the three arts of painting, music, and poetry. Principles learned from colour-music, from Pre-Raphaelite art and art-criticism, from plainchant and counterpoint in music, from Greek and Welsh studies in verse mutually enriched the poetry as well as the aesthetics behind the poetry. Hopkins was for ever reaching behind vision to theory. In his early years he turned from naturalistic idealism to set up a new Realism in Platonist terms—fixed types in a scale of nature—out of which emerged a philosophy of inscape and instress. In his maturity he developed the philosophy into a psychology, a verse theory, a theology, a moral idealism, and a Scotist scheme of salvation. Finally he speculated in the preconscious realm of memory and in number. In each case a musical metaphor lay at the base of creative vision. And at every stage of development there was renunciation and revival: when Hopkins gave up painting, he cultivated word-painting in journals; after he burnt his poetry, there was a long silence, followed by the discovery of a new verse theory; when he found poetry difficult in later years, he turned to musical composition. The death of an old art brought forth new life, and death passed into resurrection.

Vision and theory met in the interaction of poetry and spirituality, in the relationship between aesthetics and religion. Inspiration or desolation in Hopkins' prayer life gave in the poetry corresponding ejaculations of comfort or distress.[4] His stylistic habit of invocation was the natural consequence of vocation directing frequent aspirations to God. Hopkins' lifelong occupation with Greek scholarship maintained in him a Platonist view of reality, not always caught up by Scotism into a world of Christian truth, nor always turned into Christian poetry. There remained the underworld of the preconscious and primitive, ideal types and mirror images among pagan myths and Pythagorean numbers. Here in the storehouse of memory was the world of angelic possibles. It was in this way that Hopkins pursued his speculations.

What was the vision, its theory, its applications? The vision of creation was trinitarian—testifying to the fatherhood of being, the sonship of inscape, the spirituality of stress—and unitive through 'the stem of stress' or tangible finger of power in all creation. The theory centred on three key terms: inscape, the inward tongue-shape of the creature; instress, its inward stem-pressure of feeling and will; pitch, its directed singularity. The theory was extended to verse—'the inscape of spoken sound', quaint margaretting based on chime pattern and stress curvature; to human nature—a moral inscape forged by instress of will and fulfilled in the sacrificial Humanity of Christ; to psychic experience of lower heart—stress and slack of feeling, instress by association in the unconscious below reason; to the spiritual world of higher heart with levels of instress—affective will determined by nature, elective will free at pitch—and with focus on correspondence to grace in the line or stem of sequence of stress in the heart. Now, with the emergence of a doctrine of the self, with the Scotist distinction between individuality and nature, the developed theory elaborated echoes on levels of being—sakes as reflexions of individual pitch, keepings as reflexions of specific nature. Finally, the fixed points of Platonic Realism were defined in terms of Pythagorean numbers, and mathematics held out promise for a philosophical basis to metre and music. The Greek doctrine of music provided an important basis for the theory of pitch (degree of tuning on the string of being), stress (God's bow pressing on the string), and instress (man's bow responding). Yet the theory, however far abstracted, was ever brought home to the concrete through Hopkins' strong senses, his interest in primitive sensation breaking from the unconscious, in spiritualization of sensation. Furthermore, it must be remembered that the vision passed through four or five stages, that it was always in development.

These fifteen chapters have merely begun to answer many

aesthetic questions connected with Hopkins' shaping vision, but at least they have shown that vision's extension and growth from earliest to latest years. The reader of Hopkins will be able to fill in the gaps in this study as more of Hopkins' manuscripts are published from time to time. Two important tasks lie ahead: an editorial task of bringing out a complete publication of all the papers, and a critical task applied to the neglected classical notes[5] and annotated books, in which Hopkins' achievements have yet to be fairly ascertained.

NOTES AND REFERENCES

INTRODUCTION

1. Family letters, complete diaries, a new journal, more Oxford essays and spiritual notes, complete sermon-book comprise the new material. In addition to Abbott and House the editors are Graham Storey and Christopher Devlin. The life of Hopkins was undertaken by the late Humphry House and by Anthony Bischoff; publication is likely to be delayed.

2. A recent volume, *The Victorian Poets: A Guide to Research*, ed. Frederic E. Faverty (Cambridge, Mass., 1956), devotes a chapter to Hopkins as a major poet. In my estimation Hopkins deserves to rank beside Keats in the nineteenth century.

3. The Association for Promoting the Unity of Christendom.

4. Upon discovering in 1874 that Bridges wrote poetry, Hopkins resumed correspondence with a fellow poet. This fact, together with his teaching of poetry at the time, encouraged his own verse; at any rate an occasion soon arrived.

5. The story has been told and a catalogue given by Anthony Bischoff, 'The Manuscripts of Gerard Manley Hopkins', *Thought*, XXVI (1951), 551–80. I have examined Hopkins' manuscripts, as they were in 1953, at the Bodleian and at Campion Hall.

6. For names and titles see bibliography of references. John Pick gives a review of the critical writing in *The Victorian Poets*, pp. 200–7. Maurice Charney gives useful evaluations in 'A Bibliographical Study of Hopkins Criticism, 1918–1949', *Thought*, XXV (1950), 297–326.

7. See chapter 4, note 2.

8. The best treatment of Hopkins' vision to date has been given in the Scotist articles by Christopher Devlin, S.J., listed in the bibliography of references at the back of the book. Father Devlin's brilliant studies, somewhat involved in technical jargon, do not cover the early and late work before and after the Scotist phase.

CHAPTER 1

1. *Works*, ed. Cook and Wedderburn, 39 vols. (London, 1903–12), XV, 27*n.*, 91, 115. In 1857 Hopkins was at the precise age for which the *Elements* was intended—twelve or fourteen years (p. 11).

2. Newtonian optics had established the colours of the spectrum 'in proportion to one another, as the Cube-Roots of the Squares of the Numbers, $\frac{1}{2}$, $\frac{9}{16}$, $\frac{3}{5}$, $\frac{2}{3}$, $\frac{3}{4}$, $\frac{5}{6}$, $\frac{8}{9}$, 1, whereby the Lengths of a Musical Chord to sound all the Notes in an eighth are represented': Sir Isaac Newton, *Opticks: or, A Treatise of the Reflections, Refractions, Inflections & Colours of Light*, 4th ed. (1730), II. ii, p. 225; see also pp. 125–6,

Notes and References

154–6, 211–12, 295, 305, 340–1, 374. Newton's correspondence became a useful poetic device in the eighteenth century whereby light was resolved into an orderly succession of colours according to a 'symbolism of the spectrum': Marjorie Hope Nicolson, *Newton Demands the Muse: Newton's 'Opticks' and the Eighteenth Century Poets* (Princeton, 1946), p. 25; see also p. 65, n. 28: 'Newton was, of course, misled by his analogy between color and the musical chord, probably because of the influence on him of Kepler's Pythagorean devotion to the ideas of the harmony of the spheres, which is pervasive in Kepler's optical theories.' A mystical application, by which God the One was Light, represented creation as an unfolding sequence of sevenfold colour. The verse of Hopkins' father carried on the symbolism, so that it is not surprising to find Hopkins himself using the device. Hopkins' interest in Pythagorean and Platonic concepts began very early and continued to the end. For the whole subject of colour in mid-nineteenth-century art, see Ruskin. Letter III, 'On Colour and Composition', of the *Elements of Drawing* should be read in this connexion, especially pars. 152–4 (*Works*, XV, 133–6).

3. On colour-music, see the voluminous literature cited in *The Oxford Companion to Music*. On colour-concords and music of painting, see Ruskin's *Elements*, Letter III, pars. 181, 188–92, 195 (*Works*, XV, 156, 161–4, 166). By 1877–8 Ruskin could write: 'Painting is playing on a colour-violin, seventy-times-seven stringed, and inventing your tune as you play it!' and he could assert 'the existence of Colour-Law recognizable by all colourists as harmony is by all musicians'—*Laws of Fésole*, chap. vii, par. 6; chap. viii, par. 6 (*Works*, XV, 416, 432–3).

4. Hopkins commended Dixon for his line 'Vermilion, saffron, white' and noted the parallel line 'Scarlet or golden or blue' in Christina Rossetti (II. 61–2). For Ruskin, the great or sacred chord of colour was blue, purple, scarlet, white, gold: *Modern Painters*, III, Pt. IV, chap. viii, par. 9 (*Works*, V, 139); *Queen of the Air*, II, par. 95 (*Works*, XIX, 384).

5. In 1862 Hopkins was occupied in writing 'numbers of descriptions of sunrises, sunsets, sunlight' (III, 13), and as late as 1882–4 he contributed letters to the magazine *Nature* on shadow-beams and unusual colouring of volcanic sunsets (II. 161–6, Appendix II).

CHAPTER 2

1. *De Anima*, 419 a 17–20, 420 a 3–19, 425 a 2–4.

2. Intense clarity of sensation is characteristic of all Hopkins' verse: for example, 'thrush | Through the echoing timber does so rinse and wring | The ear, it strikes like lightnings to hear him sing' (No. 33).

3. *Modern Painters* II, Pt. III, Sec. ii, chap. iii (*Works*, IV, 250).

4. Ruskin's remarks are pertinent: '. . . in such a thing as the relation of position between a rainbow and the sun, there is not any definitely visible connection between them; it needs attention and calculation to discover that the center of the rainbow is the shadow of

the spectator's head'—*Modern Painters* IV, Pt. V, chap. xv, par. 33 (*Works*, VI, 276).

5. For Ruskin curvature was the universal law in all forms of beauty —*Modern Painters* II, Pt. III, Sec. i, chap. v (*Works*, IV, 88).

6. The contrast of heaven and earth was constantly used in Pre-Raphaelite verse—Rossetti's *The Blessed Damozel*, Christina Rossetti's *The Convent Threshold* to which Hopkins replied in *A Voice from the World* (No. 77). The contrast was often dramatized by choice or judgement, such as the red and blue cloths presented to Guenevere by the angel in Morris' *The Defence of Guenevere*.

7. In the *Imitatio Christi* III, 1, the door of the senses are to be shut in order to let God speak within. In 1867–8 Hopkins was picturing his inner retirement, through translations from Horace, as rejection of competitive worldliness for agrarian simplicity (Nos. 128, 129).

CHAPTER 3

1. Pater, 'Diaphaneite' (1864), *Miscellaneous Studies: A Series of Essays* (*Works*, 9 vols. [London, 1900–1], VIII, 253); 'Coleridge' (1865), *Appreciations* (*Works*, V, 68).

2. 'The School of Giorgione', *Fortnightly Review*, XXVIII (1877), 528.

3. There was talk of establishing a chair of art or aesthetics at Oxford at this time; it did not materialize until the late 1860's when the Slade Professorship was established and Ruskin was given the first appointment. See E. T. Cook, 'Introduction', Ruskin's *Works*, XX, xviii.

4. The examples chosen are Pre-Raphaelite. First of these is the chestnut-fan (IV. 55–7). For Ruskin the horse-chestnut was 'one of the crowned and lovely trees of the earth': *Modern Painters* III, Pt. IV, chap. xiv, par. 23 (*Works*, V, 265); chestnut trees appeared in Tennyson, Patmore, everywhere in the Pre-Raphaelites: see Geoffrey Grigson, 'Horse-Chestnut Trees', *The Harp of Aeolus and other Essays on Art, Literature & Nature* (London, 1948), pp. 81, 83, 84.

5. The distinction of the two kinds of beauty by use of the musical terms *chromatic* and *diatonic* is to be found in George Field, *Chromatography: or, A Treatise on Colours and Pigments and of their Powers in Painting* (London, 1835)—cited by Ruskin, *Works*, IV, 362.

6. *On the Signs of Health and Decay in the Arts*, Oxford Essays I. 6, to be published in the House–Storey edition of Hopkins' early papers.

7. Oxford Essays, IX. 3, to be published in the House–Storey edition.

CHAPTER 4

1. Compare the revelation of God's sacred name to Moses: 'I Am' or 'I will be what I will be' (Exodus iii. 14).

2. Raymond V. Schoder, S.J., Appendix to 'Interpretive Glossary

of Difficult Words in the Poems', *Immortal Diamond: Studies in Gerard Manley Hopkins*, ed. Norman Weyand, S.J. (New York, 1949), pp. 216–19, gives only one meaning for 'scape' as back-formation from 'landscape', then outlines four divisions of meaning for 'inscape': (1) intrinsic form, *forma informans*; (2) intrinsic beauty, *splendor formae*; (3) outer accidental form; (4) subjectively imposed *Gestalt* (very rare). W. A. M. Peters, S.J., *Gerard Manley Hopkins: A Critical Essay towards the Understanding of his Poetry* (London, 1948), pp. 1–2, defines inscape as a unified complex of typical characteristics of an object by which 'we may gain an insight into the individual essence of the object', or again as a 'set of individuating characteristics'. This fifth possible meaning for inscape, (5) individuating form, later associated with the Scotist *haecceitas* (Peters, p. 23), has been ably questioned and rejected by Christopher Devlin, S.J., Letter to the Editor, *Month*, N.S., IV (1950), 215. Inscape is rather typical form, the form of the naturalistic ideal, which is a fixed type. V. de S. Pinto, Letter 'Hopkins and "The Trewnesse of the Christian Religion"', *Times Literary Supplement*, 10 June 1955, p. 317, first noted the important use of 'inshape' in the Sidney–Golding translation of Philippe de Mornay's *A Woorke concerning the Trewnesse of the Christian Religion* (London, 1587), ed. Albert Feuillerat, 4 vols. (Cambridge, Eng., 1922–3). The Inshape of God's mind is the knowledge which God has of himself and is the Pattern of the world. Not only is Parmenides mentioned in connexion with 'inshape'—an important link to Hopkins' first use of inscape in a note on Parmenides—but also Plato, Pythagoras, Philo, Plotinus, Egyptians, and Jews (*Trewnesse*, III, 345–6). Such pagan anticipations—here, of the doctrine of 'three Inbeings' in the Trinity—become more significant in Hopkins' later years: see chapter 12 of this study.

3. See *OED*, 'Scape', sb. 2; 'Shape', sb. (Old English forms and meanings). 'Scape' is used as tongue of balance in Herbert's *Justice*, stanza 2.

4. Ruskin, *Elements of Drawing*, Letter I, pars. 72, 78, 96 (*Works*, XV, 67, 70, 83); Letter III, pars. 206–17 (*Works*, XV, 176–88).

5. William Barnes's 'Thoughts on Beauty and Art', *Macmillan's Magazine*, IV (1861), 126–37, illuminates the whole Pre-Raphaelite study of beauty's unfallen ideal and of God's will traced in curvature:

... the beautiful in nature is the unmarred result of God's first creative or forming will, and ... the beautiful in art is the result of an unmistaken working of man in accordance with the beautiful in nature.

... God's first formative will, then, is the fulness of every form of good, and the after work of His formative will is a filling up of the losses of good from His primary work by good of the same or other forms.

It may be said that we do not find all, or most of God's works—plants, dumb animals, or man—in the full beauty of His forming will. ...

106

Still, in plants, animals, and man, and in the world, there is yet so much of the beauty of God's primary work, that our minds can well rise from their marred shapes to the higher ones, or the beau ideal, of which they may be spoilt forms; and that beau ideal is, in our opinion, one of the true objects of high art. (pp. 126–7).

Then look for pleasure at the line of beauty, and other curves of charming grace in the wind-blown stems of grass, and bowing barley or wheat; in the water-shaken bulrush, in the leaves of plants, and in the petals of flowers; in the outlines of birds, and even their feathers and eggs; in the flowing lines of the greyhound, the horse and cat, and other animals; in the shell of the mollusc, and in the wings and markings of insects; in the swell of the downy cheek, the rounded chin, the flowing bendings of the pole and back, and the outswelling and inwinding lines from the head to the leg of woman stepping onward in the pride of youthful grace; and tell us whether nature does not show us graceful curves enough to win us from ugliness, even in a porringer.

Curves are so far in fellowship with motion that a curve may almost be taken as a symbol of it. (p. 130)

These passages clearly show the community of aesthetic idealism among Ruskin, the Pre-Raphaelites, Barnes, and Hopkins. For all, the naturalistic or beau ideal was found especially in curvature.

6. These were favoured subjects with Ruskin, who early classified unity of curvature into several kinds—subjectional, original, sequential, essential: *Modern Painters* II, Pt. III, Sec. i, chap. vi (*Works*, IV, 94–5).

7. See *OED*, 'Stress', sb., probably an aphetic form of 'distress'.

8. Coleridge's theories of the life-principle and of organic forms, set forth in *The Friend* (1809–10) and more fully in *Aids to Reflection* (1825), were remarkable anticipations of Hopkins' concepts of stress and inscape.

CHAPTER 5

1. *The Spiritual Exercises of Saint Ignatius of Loyola*, trans. with commentary and trans. of *Directorium in Exercitia* by W. H. Longridge, 4th ed. (London, 1950), pp. 184–93. The third rule applies to the pathos of tears in the next paragraph.

2. Plato in the *Republic* IV, 430d–443e, gives a tripartite division of the soul: *logos*, reason; *thymos*, spirit; *epithymos*, appetite. The chest is 'the seat of thymos' (spirit, courage, breath). Pressure on the chest forces breath out. See chapter 10 with note 4.

CHAPTER 6

1. Natural descriptions and definitions in the new journal of 1866–8 anticipate those in the journal of 1868–75, all of which it is convenient to gather together here.

Notes and References

2. For Gardner, 'quain' at first was merely a back-formation from 'quaint' (Notes, *Poems*, p. 262), later corrected to 'angular excrescences of the conventional star-shape' (Note B, *Poems and Prose of Gerard Manley Hopkins*, Penguin Poets [London, 1953], p. 243).

3. 'Pitch', an important and key word for Hopkins' vision, has both verbal force (casting or throwing in sports) and musical value (Point or elevation in tonal scale, quality of sound): see *OED*, 'Pitch', sb. 2, I and V. 'Pitch' later came to signify for Hopkins the bare self of oneness or individual being in a creature, its degree of tuning in the universe of selves: see chapter 11 with note 1.

4. See end of last paragraph in this chapter.

5. In the Oxford Note-book VII dated 1866 Hopkins inserted an autograph extract from St. Bonaventure's *Life of St. Francis*, chap. ix, translated here:

> Everything incited him to the love of God, he exulted in all the works of the Creator's hands and, by the beauty of His images, his spirit rose to their living origin and cause. He admired Supreme Beauty in all beautiful things, and by the traces impressed by God on all things he followed the Beloved. To him all creation was a stairway which led him up toward Him who is the goal of all desires. With an intensity of devotion unknown before him, he enjoyed the delights of the fount of joy in every single creature, as in rivulets flowing from it. He perceived celestial harmonies in the concord of the virtues and activities which God had given the creatures and, like the Prophet David, he was sweetly reminded by them to praise the Lord. *St. Francis of Assisi: The Legends and Lauds*, trans. N. Wydenbruck, ed. Otto Karrer (London, 1947), p. 164.

6. The divine ideas were archetypal forms contained eternally in the divine mind; these ideas of all creatures were contained in the Word (St. Augustine, *De Ideis* 2; St. Bonaventure, *Commentarii Sententiarum Petri Lombardi* I, 35, art. 1, 4). The Word as archetype of creation held an infinite number of ideas for creatures to imitate. St. Bonaventure made the doctrine of exemplarism the key and centre of metaphysics (*Collationes in Hexaëmeron* I, 13).

7. For the explanation in the following paragraph I have consulted Father Devlin's unpublished typescripts as well as published articles.

8. Hopkins would have noticed that Scotus defended Parmenides' statement against Aristotle, that all things were one being (univocal, single-worded)—not one individual but one nature (*Opus Oxoniense* I. 8, 3), and he would have recalled with a start his own note on Parmenides written in 1868 (IV. 98–102).

9. Hopkins probably translated Father Condren's hymn *O Jesu vivens in Maria* (No. 132) while at the Oratory School, 1867–8. The blue flower and blue colour have psychological and alchemical value: see C. G. Jung, *Psychology and Alchemy*, trans. R. F. C. Hull, Bollingen Series XX (New York, 1953), pp. 76–7, 203–5, referring to the

Notes and References

Theatrum Chemicum and to Guillaume de Digulleville, *Les pélerinages de la vie humaine, de l'âme, et de Jésus Christ.*

CHAPTER 7

1. Hopkins explained that there were two kinds of accent—tonic degree, centre of illumination, pitch, and emphatic weight, centre of gravity, stress (IV. 223–4).
2. See the curvature visibly traced out in diagrams of verse rhythm (IV. 240).
3. At this point a recommendation may be made for a variorum edition of the poems, to include the text with all variants on one leaf and the text scored for performance on the opposite leaf. Readers and listeners would thus be encouraged to understand how the poems should sound.

CHAPTER 8

1. The Franciscan spirit of the Jesuit Hopkins is to be found in St. Ignatius, father-founder of the Society of Jesus. The *Spiritual Exercises* follows the affective tradition of the Franciscans, in spite of subsequent Jesuit developments. Consult Henri Bremond, *Histoire Littéraire du Sentiment Religieux en France Depuis la Fin des Guerres de Religion Jusqu'à Nos Jours*, 12 vols. (Paris, 1920–36), II, 137–8; III, 29–31n., Appendice 2; V, 43, 267–8, 277, 307; VIII, 189n.
2. In Pindar's Olympian Ode XIV, 12, God is called 'ever-flowing': 'the Olympian Father's glory that flows like a river from age to age'. In a retreat note of 1881 Hopkins used an image similar to that here in the *Deutschland*:

    Time has 3 dimensions and one positive pitch or direction. It is therefore not so much like any river or any sea as like the Sea of Galilee, which has the Jordan running through it and giving a current to the whole. (IV. 343)

3. Scotus, *Opus Oxoniense*, IV. 10, 4.
4. 'Beyond saying sweet, past telling of tongue' (stanza 9. 5) echoes Herbert's *The Banquet*, 'Passeth tongue to taste or tell'.
5. The two great saints of conversion made voyages and so take up their places fittingly in an ode of the sea.
6. The false ship may stand for Protestantism ('O Deutschland, double a desperate name!'—stanza 20. 3), the true ship of souls for the Roman Catholic Church (the 'ark' of stanza 33. 2). There is the same symbolism in *The Loss of the Eurydice* (No. 41), 'Fast foundering own generation' (1. 88).
7. The nun's cry was literally reproduced from the London *Times* account (Norman Weyand, 'The Historical Basis of *The Wreck of the Deutschland* and *The Loss of the Eurydice*', *Immortal Diamond*, p. 368). *Maranatha*, 'O Lord, come', has been the cry of the saints through the ages.

8. The climactic vision of an angelic Christ has already been prepared for in stanzas 2, 3, 21. Here the Presence is parallel to the flush of sacramental grace in stanzas 7–8. These two climaxes are similar acts of grace, each four-fifths of the way through the ode (8 in 10 and 28 in 35), a coincidental ratio interesting in view of Hopkins' gathering interest in such things (see chapter 13).

9. In Plato's *Symposium* 206, love is birth, creation, power of conception and parturition. As Plato's idea of beauty presides at the birth of love, so Christ as absolute Beauty presides over his birth in the heart. 'Created being' and 'being created' are reciprocal activities in Scotus and Hopkins.

CHAPTER 9

1. For application of the senses, note the comments in the *Spiritual Exercises* and *Directorium*, pp. 93–5, 314–15: *Exercises*, second week, first day, fifth contemplation; *Directorium*, chap. xx. For visionary sensation, see the lucid explanation by Christopher Devlin, 'An Essay on Scotus', *Month*, CLXXXII (1946), 456–66.

2. *Phaedrus* 251.

3. Jean Daniélou, *Platonisme et Théologie Mystique: Essai sur la Doctrine Spirituelle de Saint Grégoire de Nysse* (Paris, 1944), p. 272:

Il faut que l'âme soit complètement harnachée (par les vertus) pour pouvoir recevoir le roi comme cavalier. Peu importe que celui-ci soit représenté comme montant sur le cheval, ou comme se trouvant en nous, pour y demeurer et y circuler et pénétrer dans les profondeurs de notre âme. C'est en effet la même chose qu'avoir Dieu en soi et sur soi. . . . Tu deviendras par la foi la monture et l'habitacle de celui qui veut reposer en toi par son habitation en toi. (XLIV, 820A; 821A)

4. The inscape is the realm of Christ: 'kingdom of daylight's dauphin' is echoed by a later line, 'Realm both Christ is heir to and there reigns' (No. 47, l. 32).

5.
    Soul of Christ, sanctify me.
    Body of Christ, save me.
    Blood of Christ, inebriate me.
    Water from the side of Christ, wash me.
    Passion of Christ, strengthen me.
    O good Jesu, hear me.
    Within thy wounds hide me.
    Suffer me not to be separated from thee.
    From the malicious enemy defend me.
    In the hour of my death call me
    And bid me come to thee,
    That with thy saints I may praise thee
    For ever and ever. Amen.

6. The inscape in the outspread bird is the cross. The plough is the cross acting in the field of the heart. The cross-plough is familiar in emblem-literature (Francis Quarles, *The School of the Heart*, 'The Tilling of the Heart'). Another poem of the period (*The Caged Skylark*, No. 39) also shows emblem-influence (Quarles, *Emblems Divine and Moral*, Book V, Emblem 10: 'My soul is like a bird, my flesh the cage').

7. It is an interesting coincidence that Ruskin in his diary of 1875 observed the two modes of stopping of the windhover (*Works*, XXIV, xxix). For the flight of the windhover, see also *Deucalion* II, i, 18 (*Works*, XXVI, 305). Exact observations on the flight of birds were made by Leonardo da Vinci, *The Notebooks*, trans. Edward MacCurdy, 2 vols. (London, 1938); these well serve to explain the swing, hurl, and rebuff of the windhover's flight:

If the bird which does not beat its wings should not wish to descend rapidly to a depth, then after a certain amount of slanting descent it will set itself to rise by a reflex movement and to revolve in a circle. . . . (I, 454)

For a simple circular rise,

. . . they travel above the flight of the wind, and at the end of it (that is, the end of the flight) turn and face the direction of the wind, receiving its buffetting from beneath, and so finish the reverse movement against the wind. (I, 455)

When the bird is driven by the wind it proceeds continually to descend by a slanting movement, and when it desires to rise to its former height it turns backwards and uses the impetus of the wind as a wedge. (I, 481)

8. See chapter 6 with note 5. The stairway or ladder of creation is best seen in the late sonnet *Heraclitean Fire* (No. 72), discussed in chapter 14 with note 5.

9. Fires, saps, and songs were Platonic in origin, though Christian in Hopkins' use of them. In the *Timaeus* (45B and C, 58C, 67C and D) Plato's mechanism of vision involves three kinds of fire or light: (1) daylight, a body of pure fire diffused into the air by the sun; (2) the visual current, a pure fire contained in the eyeball and capable of streaming out towards the object seen; (3) the colour of the external object, a flame streaming off from every body. In the *Timaeus* (59E–60B) Plato has a theory of saps—wine that warms, oil that smooths and glistens, honey that relaxes and sweetens, verjuice that burns. Musical songs are especially Platonic.

10. Aristotle, *De Sensu*, 437 b 23 ff.; Plato, *Timaeus*, 45C. There is a similar use of Empedoclean doctrine of sight in No. 50, first quatrain.

11. Keble, *Praelectiones Academicae*, I, 22; II, 222: a poetic theory of catharsis, healing, and self-revelation of the poet.

12. In the fall of 1877 Hopkins, corresponding with John Rhys about Welsh verse, suggested that Welsh chime was reducible to one Celtic trait (III. 416).

Notes and References

CHAPTER 10

1. Note the intensification towards increasing fixity in the succession of physical objects ('bow or brooch or braid or brace, lace, latch or catch or key') with repeated vowels ($\bar{o}$, $\bar{a}$, $\breve{a}$, $\bar{e}$). Relevant in this connection is Hopkins' note on Lancashire gardeners saying Ay:

> What the one says the other assents to by the roots and upwards from the level of the sea. He makes a kind of Etna of assent, without effort but with a long fervent breathing out of all the breath there is in him. The word runs through the whole scale of the vowels beginning broad in the barrel of the waist and ending fine on the drop of the lip. . . . It is equal to about four semibreves and morsels itself into vibrations like echos under a bridge and dying off like tufts of smoke against a ribbed vaulting. (III. 114).

2. Hopkins explained to Bridges:

> You must know that words like *charm* and *enchantment* will not do: the thought is of beauty that can be physically kept and lost and by physical things only, like keys; then the things must come from the *mundus muliebris*; and thirdly they must not be markedly oldfashioned. You will see that this limits the choice of words very much indeed. (I. 161–2)

3. There is a correspondence here to the three moments of stress worked out in the *Deutschland*: feeling / affliction; aspiration / election; spirit / elevation. See chapter 8.

4. *Phaedrus* 245–6.

5. *The Candle Indoors,* companion sonnet to *The Lantern out of Doors,* used the same Empedoclean doctrine of vision—beams of fire wavering through moisture. See chapter 9 with note 9.

6. For Hopkins each poet or artist was like a species in nature (III. 370), like an angel in traditional theology.

7. Species, a distinct class in logic and philosophy, an idea in Platonism, reflexion or visible form in common usage—and not, for Hopkins, a biological class in natural history.

8. Hopkins defined 'sake' as 'the being a thing has outside itself, as a voice by its echo, a face by its reflection, a body by its shadow, a man by his name, fame, or memory, *and also* . . . something distinctive, marked, specifically or individually speaking . . .' (I. 83). 'Sakes' of Purcell were accidentals in the musical inscape.

9. The *haecceitas* ('thisness', the fulfilment of individual degree) was in the inscape, but not identified with it. Inscape was equivalent to Scotus' *species specialissima* (nature being created in most specific type on verge of individuation, yet not isolated as an individual from the pattern). See chapter 6 and consult Christopher Devlin, 'The Image and the Word—II', *Month*, N.S.; III (1950), 197–201; Letter to the Editor, *Month*, N.S., IV (1950), 213–15. See chapter 11 for 'pitch' as *haecceitas*, with note 1.

10. For Bridges, see I. 72, 96, 98; II. 74–6. For Dixon, see I. 139; II. 20, 37, 55–6, 61–2.

CHAPTER 11

1. The word 'pitch' had already been used in the journals: see chapter 6 with note 3. *Haecceitas* was identified with *arbitrium*, 'moral pitch' (IV. 322, 328).

2. The application and warning are clearer in No. 112: 'There is your world within. | There rid the dragons, root out there the sin.'

3. Hopkins' distinction between affective and elective will may have been derived from his experience of Ignatian prayer, which is divided into colloquies (exercises of affections) and resolutions (exercises of elections). But it is intellectualized by the Scotist distinction between personality (spontaneous fulfilment) and individuality (completion by opposition or bracing).

4. Similarly in *Binsey Poplars* (No. 43), the hewing down of object-inscapes meant more than loss of beauty to the subject; it meant loss of vision, of the eye itself.

5. The three freedoms of pitch, play, and field correspond to the three terms of the word, prepossession, definition, and extension. See chapter 4.

6. 'Scope' along with 'scape' was a word of great importance to Hopkins in 1887 when he was searching dictionaries for meanings; 'scope' meant freedom of action or play, corresponding to the 'scape' or nature within which it played or exercised. See III. 284–6.

7. Note the sound-colour analogy of the first three lines. Relevant to the sonnet No. 57 is the concept of 'sake' as 'the being a thing has outside itself', used in No. 45. See chapter 10 with note 8.

8. This order links back, on quite another level, to the *Deutschland*: 'His mystery must be instressed, stressed'—elected by faith, acted out by imitation (No. 28, stanza 5. 7).

9. Here Hopkins followed Marie Lataste: it is not grace that makes saints, but correspondence to grace, and this correspondence is a grace, the grace of graces also coming from God and never refused when asked for. See *The Letters and Writings of Marie Lataste*, trans. Edward Healy, eds. two Fathers of the Society of Jesus, 3 vols. (London, 1893–4), I, 52.

10. See chapter 6 for 'cleave' and the use of 'divine' geometry.

11. Omitting the moment of creative stress which is not felt, the other moments of stress in the notes are redemptive or corrective stress / affliction, and elevating stress / elevation, between which comes the bare acknowledgement / aspiration, an instress. Notice that what is kept vague and implicit in the ode is made explicit in the notes: the activities of the three Persons of the Godhead giving grace to the soul.

12. Father Roothaan's edition of the *Exercitia Spiritualia* (Paris, 1865) was part of the established Jesuit scholarship which obscured the Franciscan origins of the *Exercises*. See chapter 8, note 1. Note that the Jesuit tradition of Suarism was half-way between Thomism and Scotism. Yet Hopkins was isolated as a Scotist; he met the only two other Scotists in England in one week in 1874 (IV. 198).

CHAPTER 12

1. Foremost were studies in Greek for a work on the art of the Greek lyric poets and Pindar, on the Dorian measure and other metres (I. 150, 228–9, 246–7; II. 150; III. 252–3, 276, 374, 377). Materials were collected for prospective studies of Homer, Aeschylus, Sophocles, Aristophanes (III. 257; I. 225, 266, 277; G. F. Lahey, *Gerard Manley Hopkins* [London, 1930], p. 144). He also proposed philosophical papers on the Greek negatives, the Argei, statistics and free will, light and the ether, as well as reviews of the poetry of Bridges and of Patmore (I. 270, 303, 291–2; II. 139; I. 241; III. 389). He hoped to prepare a critical edition of St. Patrick's Confession (I. 195). He speculated in etymologies, attempting to derive names and titles of Greek deities from Egyptian originals; consulted authorities on Welsh mutations, Scotus' birthplace, Loisette's mneumonic system, Skeat's derivations; and collected notes for a work on British dialects (III. 257–92, 414–25, 431–2; Lahey, ibid.; Plures, 'Father Gerard Hopkins—III', *Dublin Review*, CLXVII (1920), 54).

2. The distinction is made clear by Jacques Maritain, *Creative Intuition in Art and Poetry* (London, 1953), pp. 91–2:

There are two kinds of unconscious, two great domains of psychological activity screened from the grasp of consciousness: the preconscious of the spirit in its living springs, and the unconscious of blood and flesh, instincts, tendencies, complexes, repressed images and desires, traumatic memories, as constituting a closed or autonomous dynamic whole.

Hopkins was concerned with both kinds of unconscious, at first with the automatic unconscious of physic existence (chapter 5), later with the musical preconscious of spiritual essence (chapter 12). The Scotist distinction between individuality and common nature allowed for two levels in the unconscious—roughly equivalent to Jung's distinction between the personal level of individual memory and the common or shared level of racial memory.

3. In notes for the commentary dated 1881 (IV. 346, 350), Hopkins interpreted the earth and the constellation Draco, in terms of the woman and the dragon of the Apocalypse (Revelation xii)—which would make the constellation Perseus equivalent to St. Michael. Perseus in No. 49 is usually identified as Christ (Gardner, Notes, *Poems* p. 236), but this identification may be mistaken. St. Michael (or Christ 'steaded' in St. Michael) seems to be intended. Another possibility for Perseus is St. George of England. At this time, 1879, Ruskin represented St. George of the Guild as Perseus in the fight against industrialism: see 'The Place of Dragons', chap. xi of *St. Mark's Rest* (*Works*, XXIV, 377).

4. Among Jesuit rules for professors of rhetoric, the subject of the Sibyls is considered an acceptable topic for prelections: see *St. Ignatius and the Ratio Studiorum*, ed. Edward A. Fitzpatrick (New York, 1933), p. 215. The Sibyl (from *Aeneid* VI) is the will of God, an oracle speak-

ing through the heart and interpreting the vision. For a full account of No. 62, see chapter 11.

5. The 'grey eye' is the steersman, reason—a common epithet in Greek for wisdom (applied by Homer to Odysseus and Athena). Aristotle compares the soul's control of the body with a pilot's steering of a ship (*De Anima* I. i).

6. See chapter 10 with note 8.

7. See chapter 10 with notes 7 and 9.

8. A. Loisette, *The Loisettian School of Physiological Memory* (London, n.d.), cites testimonials of 1885–6 from the headmaster of Roehampton and from the rector of Stonyhurst (pp. 8, 40), two Jesuit houses which Hopkins visited. For details of the system, see A. Loisette, *Assimilative Memory: or, How to Attend and Never Forget* (London, 1896): the three laws of memory (pp. 3–4), making the intellect stay with the senses by force of will (pp. 17–20), analytic substitutions for dates and figures (p. 66). For an appraisal and criticism of Loisette's system, see A. E. Middleton, *Memory Systems New and Old*, enlarged with G. S. Fellows, *Bibliography of Mneumonics 1325–1888* (New York, 1888), pp. 96–8, 114.

CHAPTER 13

1. Both Hopkins and Herbert were fascinated with numbers and proportion, a mathematical bias evident in their verse architecture. While Herbert employed the counterpoint of short lines against long lines, Hopkins exploited the stress counterpoint of abrupt and outriding feet within long lines. Both poets observed rigid patterns— Herbert rendering physical arrangement of the poem on the page significant, but Hopkins depending almost entirely on the ear to render dynamics of syntax intelligible.

2. Hopkins probably consulted James Hadley, *Essays Philosophical and Critical Selected from the Papers of* (London, 1873): see p. 107 for ratio of 4 : 3 in irrational feet.

3. To trace the beginnings and later history of number theories, consult Vincent Foster Hopper, *Medieval Number Symbolism: Its Sources, Meaning, and Influence on Thought and Expression* (New York, 1938). For St. Augustine, see chap. v. The number 1 is God, Jehovah; the triad is the Holy Trinity; the diad is the dual nature of Christ in the Trinity; 5 stands for the five wounds; from the triune principle of God and the quadruple principle of man are produced the universal symbols 7 and 12 (pp. 78–86). Notice how this numerology corresponds to that of the *Deutschland* (No. 28): 'Five!' as the number of the stigmata (stanza 22); 'Mid-numbered He in three of the thunder-throne!' for the dual Christ in the Trinity (stanza 34. 5). It should be noted that Scotus took over through Avicenna the Platonic theory of number. Hopkins' interest in numbers began at home. His father was head of a firm of average adjusters and published *A Handbook of Average* (1857) and *The Cardinal Numbers* (1887), to the latter of which

Hopkins contributed. The Pythagorean bias in Hopkins can be traced back to the Platonic Realism of mathematical and musical bases and to such a journal-entry as that of 1871 where the unusual series 1, 2, 4, 8 is noted in architectural subdivisions (IV. 154–5). The principle of harmonic proportion in architecture was a Pre-Raphaelite musical reading: see William Barnes, Letter, *Gentleman's Magazine*, N.S., XX (1843), 574–5.

4. On the principles of Pythagoreanism, consult Aristotle, *Metaphysics* 985 b 23 ff. See also the Pythagorean influence in Plato: analysis of the world's contents (*Philebus* 16c–17a, 23c ff.), the *psyche-harmonia* argument (*Phaedo*, 85e ff.), the doctrine of *anamnesis* (*Meno* 81a ff., *Phaedo* 70c ff., 72e ff., *Phaedrus* 248a ff., *Republic* 614b ff., *Timaeus* 41a ff.), creation (*Timaeus* 53c, 55–6), the birth-number (*Republic* 546b–c).

5. Hopkins was conducting an intensive analysis of likely dialect words in the dictionaries, such as Wright's and Skeat's. 'Scope' was one of the words (III. 284–6).

6. For quain, see chapter 6 with note 2.

7. The Pythagorean doctrine of the harmony of the spheres is set forth in Aristotle, *De Caelo* 290 b 12. For a contemporary account of Pythagorean and Greek music theory based on numbers, see W[illiam] Chappell, *The History of Music (Art and Science)* (London, 1874), pp. 58–9, 76–7, 86–7, 206–7, 381–3.

8. The musical authorities include a friend of Bridges (name deleted by Bridges), Sir F. Gore Ouseley, Sir Robert Stewart, H. E. Woolridge, W. S. Rockstro.

CHAPTER 14

1. St. Ignatius' 'Kingdom of Christ' (*Spiritual Exercises*, second week) is one source of No. 63. Another source is the Florentine legend of St. Giovanni Gualberto, represented in Burne-Jones' painting *The Merciful Knight* (1863), which shows an effigy of Christ bending down from a wayside crucifix to embrace a kneeling knight. See Percy H. Bate, *The English Pre-Raphaelite Painters, their Associates and Successors* (London, 1899), illus. opp. p. 104, and p. 105, for reproduction and for account of the legend, the probable source of the scene in the sestet.

2. For spiritual desolation, read the fourth to ninth Rules for the Discernment of Spirits (*Spiritual Exercises*, pp. 186–8).

3. For the cliff, compare Aeschylus, *Supplices*, 792–9.

4. 'Bones built in me, flesh filled, blood brimmed the curse' (No. 69) reverses 'Thou hast bound bones and veins in me, fastened me flesh' (No. 28, stanza 1. 5).

5. In curtal sonnet No. 46, Patience given to the soul is expected to grow up into Peace; in No. 70, Patience means war, not peace, yet allows peaceful healing.

6. See chapter 6 with note 5.

Notes and References

7. St. Bonaventure, *Commentarii Sententiarum Petri Lombardi* I. 3. 1. 1. 2. fund. 4; I. 3. 1. un. ad 4; II. 16. 1. 1. conclusio; *Breviloquium* II. 12. 1; *Itinerarium mentis ad Deum* I. 2; *Collationes in Hexaëmeron* II. 20 ff. There were an infinite number of degrees of analogy between creatures and God, but three general grades—shadow (distant and confused), vestige (distant and distinct), image (near and distinct). See also the *De Imitatio Christi* II. 8.

8. Clouds are referred to as armies or hosts in Pindar, *Pythian Ode* VI. 10 ff.

9. Hopkins associated the cross with the sea-beacon in wayside crucifixes of Europe (IV. 107). In emblem-literature the body is a ship carrying the soul and foundering in the sea of the world, while the Lord waits in the port to receive the soul (Quarles, *Emblems Divine and Moral*, Book III, Emblem 11).

CHAPTER 15

1. The Romantic rediscovery of 'sympathies', alchemical or psychic affinities in metals and plants, of correspondences between sound and colour, may be related to Hopkins' sympathetic analogies. There was a difference in Hopkins: the Scotist doctrine of the univocity of being by which all creatures shared common nature in levels or degrees summed up in Christ.

2. Consult E. D. H. Johnson, *The Alien Vision of Victorian Poetry: Sources of the Poetic Imagination in Tennyson, Browning, and Arnold* (Princeton, 1952), for the relationship of the poets to their society. For a criticism of Johnson's view, see J. H. Buckley, 'General Matrials', *The Victorian Poets*, pp. 22–3.

3. Influence on Hopkins of the baroque verse of the seventeenth century began with his reading of Herbert as well as of the recent Church school (John Keble, Isaac Williams, Christina Rossetti). The Anglo-Catholics were aware of baroque emblems: the *Pia Desideria* was mentioned, for example, by John Mason Neale, trans., *Hymns Chiefly Mediaeval, on the Joys and Glories of Paradise* (London, 1865), p. 90. Baroque influence on Hopkins continued no doubt with his perusal of Jesuit emblem-books. For instance, he knew the life of St. Stanislaus 'commented on under emblems . . . much in the style of Herbert and his school and about that date' (I. 95). Under the twelfth rule for professors of rhetoric in the *Ratio Studiorum*, there are subjects to be found 'Also in hieroglyphics, Pythagorean symbols, apothegms, adages, emblems and enigmas' (*St. Ignatius and the Ratio Studiorum*, p. 214). Now much of Hopkins' imagery may be understood through study of baroque emblem-literature, repository of classical and biblical symbols (winged bird-soul, heart, candle, scales, lace, ship, sea, harvest, plant, time, death, water, fire). Baroque architecture—a coiling motion yearning for the infinite, yet held within a rigid framework of the finite, an energy blending into contrasts of convex and concave

117

and shining in contrasts of light and dark—does offer striking parallels to Hopkins' style.

4. The classical treatise in this connexion is Henri Bremond, *Prière et poésie* (Paris, 1926), trans. Algar Thorold (London, 1927). Using Paul Claudel's distinction between *animus* (the surface self of the classicists) and *anima* (the deeper self of the Romanticists), together with Bergson's distinction between abstract intellect and living intuition, Abbé Bremond confined poetry to the expression of *anima*, the intuitive heart of St. Augustine and Pascal. He also suggested that poetry was a preliminary sketch or revelation of mystical experience, that the poet was a half saint who told mystical secrets and dispersed the spring of prayer at its source. This thesis will not do for Hopkins, because as the latter well knew intellectual exertion in verse rhetoric was necessary to complete inspiration. Bremond took account of inspiration only, Hopkins of stress and inscape.

5. Here Peters, pp. 148–9, has led the way with commentary on Hopkins' Homer notes.

LIST OF WORKS CITED

A. HOPKINS' WORKS

Poems of Gerard Manley Hopkins, third edition, the first edition with preface and notes by Robert Bridges enlarged and edited with notes and a biographical introduction by W. H. Gardner, fifth impression revised with additional poems. London, 1956.

Poems and Prose of Gerard Manley Hopkins, selected with an introduction and notes by W. H. Gardner. Penguin Poets D 15. London, 1953.

The Letters of Gerard Manley Hopkins to Robert Bridges, edited with notes and an introduction by Claude Colleer Abbott. London, 1935, 1955—cited as I.

The Correspondence of Gerard Manley Hopkins and Richard Watson Dixon, edited with notes and an introduction by Claude Colleer Abbott. London, 1935, 1955.—cited as II.

Further Letters of Gerard Manley Hopkins Including His Correspondence with Coventry Patmore, edited with notes and an introduction by Claude Colleer Abbott, second edition revised and enlarged. London, 1956.—cited as III.

The Note-Books and Papers of Gerard Manley Hopkins, edited with notes and an introduction by Humphry House. London, 1937. —cited as IV.

B. SECONDARY WORKS

Aeschylus, translated into English prose by F. A. Paley, second edition revised and corrected. London, 1871.

Aristotle, *Works*, translated and edited by J. A. Smith and W. D. Ross, 12 volumes. Oxford, 1908–52.

St. [Aurelius] Augustinus, *Works*, translated and edited by J. H. S. Burleigh, A. C. Outler, John Burnaby. 3 volumes. Library of Christian Classics. London, 1953–5.

    Basic Writings, edited by Whitney J. Oates. 2 volumes. New York, 1948.

Barnes, William, Letter, *Gentleman's Magazine*, N.S., XX (1843), 574–5.

    'Thoughts on Beauty and Art', *Macmillan's Magazine*, IV (1861), 126–37.

Bate, Percy H., *The English Pre-Raphaelite Painters: their Associates and Successors*. London, 1899.

Bischoff, D. Anthony, S.J., 'The Manuscripts of Gerard Manley Hopkins', *Thought*, XXV (1951), 551–80.

St. Bonaventura, *Opera Omnia*, edited by Quaracchi. 10 volumes. Florence, 1882–1902.

List of Works Cited

Brémond, Henri, *Histoire Littéraire du Sentiment Religieux en France Depuis la Fin des Guerres de Religion Jusqu'à Nos Jours.* 12 volumes. Paris, 1920–36.

—— *Prière et Poésie.* Paris, 1926. *Prayer & Poetry: A Contribution to Poetical Theory*, translated by Algar Thorold. London, 1927.

Chappell, W[illiam], *The History of Music (Art and Science).* London, [1874].

Charney, Maurice, 'A Bibliographical Study of Hopkins Criticism, 1918–1949', *Thought*, XXV (1950), 297–326.

Daniélou, Jean, *Platonisme et Théologie Mystique: Essai sur la Doctrine Spirituelle de Saint Grégoire de Nysse.* Paris, 1944.

D'Arcy, Martin C., S.J., 'Gerard Manley Hopkins', *Great Catholics*, edited by Claude Williamson, O.S.C. New York, 1941. Pages 358–66.

—— 'Gerard Manley Hopkins', *Month*, CLXXXI (1945), 67–9.

da Vinci, Leonardo, *The Notebooks*, translated by Edward MacCurdy. 2 volumes. London, 1938.

Devlin, Christopher, S.J., 'An Essay on Scotus', *Month*, CLXXXII (1946), 456–66.

—— 'Hopkins and Duns Scotus', *New Verse*, No. 14 (April 1935), 12–17.

—— 'The Ignatian Inspiration of Gerard Hopkins', *Blackfriars*, XVI (1935), 887–900.

—— 'The Image and the Word', *Month*, N.S., III (1950), 114–27, 191–202.

—— Letter to the Editor, *Month*, N.S., IV (1950), 213–15.

—— *The Psychology of Duns Scotus.* London Aquinas Society. Oxford, 1950.

—— 'Time's Eunuch', *Month*, N.S., I (1949), 303–12.

Field, George, *Chromotography: or, A Treatise on Colours and Pigments and of their Powers in Painting.* London, 1835.

St. Francis of Assisi: The Legends and Lauds, translated by N. Wydenbruck, edited by Otto Karrer. London, 1947.

Gardner, W[illiam] H[enry], *Gerard Manley Hopkins (1844–1889): A Study of Poetic Idiosyncrasy in Relation to Poetic Tradition.* 2 volumes. I, second revised edition, London, 1948. II, first edition, 1949.

Grigson, Geoffrey, *The Harp of Aeolus and other Essays on Art, Literature & Nature.* London, 1948.

Hadley, James, *Essays Philosophical and Critical Selected from the Papers of.* London, 1873.

Herbert, George, *The Poetical Works*, edited by Charles Cowden Clarke. London, 1863.

Hogarth, William, *The Analysis of Beauty, Written with a View of Fixing the Fluctuating Ideas of Taste.* London, n.d.

Hopper, Vincent Foster, *Medieval Number Symbolism: Its Sources, Meaning, and Influence on Thought and Expression.* New York, 1938.

List of Works Cited

St. Ignatius and the Ratio Studiorum, edited by Edward A. Fitzpatrick. New York, 1933.

St. Ignatius of Loyola, *Exercitia Spiritualia cum Versione Litterali ex Autographo Hispanico* [edited by Father Roothaan]. Paris, 1865.

    The Spiritual Exercises translated from the Spanish with a commentary and a translation of *the Directorium in Exercitia* by W. H. Longridge, S.S.J.E., fourth edition. London, 1950.

Immortal Diamond: Studies in Gerard Manley Hopkins, edited by Norman Weyand, S.J. New York, 1949.

Johnson, E. D. H., *The Alien Vision of Victorian Poetry: Sources of the Poetic Imagination in Tennyson, Browning, and Arnold.* Princeton, 1952.

Jung, C. G., *Psychology and Alchemy,* translated by R. F. C. Hull. Bollingen Series XX. New York, 1953. In *Collected Works of C. G. Jung,* Volume 12.

Keble, John, *Praelectiones Academicae Oxonii Habitae, 1832–1841.* 2 volumes. Oxford, 1844. *Keble's Lectures on Poetry 1832–1841,* translated by Edward Kershaw Francis. 2 volumes. Oxford, 1912.

The Kenyon Critics, *Gerard Manley Hopkins.* New Directions Books. Norfolk, Connecticut, 1945.

Lahey, G. F., S.J., *Gerard Manley Hopkins.* London, 1930.

Lataste, Marie, C.S.H., *The Letters and Writings,* translated by Edward Healy, edited by two Fathers of the Society of Jesus. 3 volumes. London, 1893–4.

Loisette, A[lphonse] [Marcus Dwight Larrowe], *Assimilative Memory: or, How to Attend and Never Forget.* London, 1896.

    The Loisettian School of Physiological Memory. London, n.d.

Maritain, Jacques, *Creative Intuition in Art and Poetry.* London, 1954.

Middleton, A. E., *Memory Systems New and Old,* enlarged with G. S. Fellows, *Bibliography of Mneumonics 1325–1888.* New York, 1888.

Neale, J[ohn] M[ason], translator and editor, *Hymns, Chiefly Mediaeval, on the Joys and Glories of Paradise.* London, 1865.

Newton, Sir Isaac, *Opticks: or, A Treatise of the Reflections, Refractions, Inflections & Colours of Light,* fourth edition. 1730. Reprinted New York, 1931.

New Verse, No. 14. April, 1935.

Nicolson, Marjorie Hope, *Newton Demands the Muse: Newton's 'Opticks' and the Eighteenth Century Poets.* Princeton, 1946.

The Oxford Companion to Music, edited by Percy A. Scholes, ninth edition, London, 1955.

The Oxford English Dictionary, edited by Sir James A. H. Murray, Henry Bradley, W. A. Craigie, C. T. Onions. 10 volumes and supplement. Oxford, 1888–1933.

Pater, Walter H., 'The School of Giorgione', *Fortnightly Review,* XXVIII (1877), 526–38.

List of Works Cited

Pater, Walter H., *Works*, 9 volumes. London, 1900–1.

Peters, W. A. M., S.J., *Gerard Manley Hopkins: A Critical Essay towards the Understanding of his Poetry*. London, 1948.

Pick, John, *Gerard Manley Hopkins: Priest and Poet*. London, 1942.

Pindarus, *Works*, translated with literary and critical commentaries by Lewis Richard Farnell. 3 volumes. London, 1930–2.

Pinto, V. de S., Letter 'Hopkins and "The Trewnesse of the Christian Religion" ', *Times Literary Supplement*, 10 June 1955, page 317.

Plato, *The Dialogues*, translated by B[enjamin] Jowett, third edition. 5 volumes. London, 1892.

Quarles, Francis, *Emblems, Divine and Moral; The School of the Heart; and Hieroglyphics of the Life of Man*, a new edition [by W. W.]. London, 1866.

Ruskin, John, *Works*, Library Edition, edited by E. T. Cook and Alexander Wedderburn. 39 volumes. London, 1903–12.

Scotus, Joannes Duns, *Opera Omnia*, edited by Wadding. 12 volumes. Paris, 1891–5.

Sidney, Sir Philip, and Arthur Golding, translators, *A Woorke concerning the trewnesse of the Christian Religion*, written in French by Philip of Mornay. London, 1587. In Volume III, pages 247–367, of Sidney's *Complete Works*, edited by Albert Feuillerat. 4 volumes. Cambridge, England, 1922–3.

St. Thomas à Kempis, *The Imitation of Christ*, facsimile reproduction of the first edition printed at Augsburg, 1471–2, introduction by W. J. K. Little. London, 1893.

The Victorian Poets: A Guide to Research, edited by Frederic E. Faverty. Cambridge, Massachusetts, 1956.

INDEX

Abbott, Claude Colleer, 1, 103
Aeschylus, 75, 114, 116
Aesthetics, 18, 19, 20, 21, 22, 99
Alexandrine, 62, 82, 83, 93, 98
Allegory, 11, 75, 77-9
Analogy, 10, 20, 34, 78-9, 117
Andromeda, 77, 78
Angels, 60, 62, 67, 72, 73, 76, 77, 79, 85, 92, 95, 98, 100, 110, 112
Anglo-Catholicism, 2, 17, 95, 117
Apollo, 93
Arbitrium, 67, 68, 69, 113
Archbolds. 92
Architecture, 15, 20, 21, 116
Aristophanes, 114
Aristotle, 14, 18, 42, 108, 111, 115, 116
Arnold, Matthew, 2, 96
Art, 9, 12, 14, 15, 18, 20, 22, 42, 63, 69, 75, 79, 81, 82, 84, 87, 95
Association for Promoting the Unity of Christendom, 2, 103
Athena, 115
Augustine, St., 7, 37, 45, 52, 53, 78, 82, 83, 84, 94, 108, 115, 118
Avicenna, 115

Balliol College, 2
Barnes, William, 63, 79, 106-7
Baroque, 78, 96-7, 117
Bate, Percy H., 116
Beauty, 9, 15, 18-22, 26, 38, 41, 54, 58, 59, 64, 106, 107, 108, 113
Benlowes, Edward, 96
Bergson, Henri, 118
Birds, 9, 12, 13, 52-3, 54, 60, 61, 62, 98, 111, 117
Bischoff, D. Anthony, S.J., 103
Blessed Sacrament, 29, 38, 44-5, 50, 52, 58, 76, 90
Blessed Virgin, 47, 57, 67, 76, 78, 89, 95
Blow, John, 86
Bodleian Library, 4, 103
Bonaventure, St., 37, 94, 108, 117
Bremond, Henri, 109, 118
Bridges, Robert, 1, 3, 4, 5, 62, 63, 93, 103, 112, 114, 116
Browning, Robert, 2, 96

Buckley, J. H., 117
Burne-Jones, Edward B., 116

Campion Hall, 5, 103
Caradoc, 68, 88
Carlyle, Thomas, 78
Chappell, William, 116
Charney, Maurice, 103
Chesterfield, 3
Chime, 40-1, 43, 55, 56, 79, 100
Chords, 6, 11, 21, 42
Christ, 29, 37-9, 43-9, 50, 52, 53, 55, 57, 58, 59, 65, 66, 70, 71, 72, 76, 77, 79, 80, 88, 89, 90, 91, 92, 93, 94, 95, 100, 110, 114, 115, 116, 117
Chromatic beauty, 20, 21, 27, 41, 42, 105
Church, 57, 58, 77, 88, 117
Church of England, 17
Church of Rome, 2, 17, 77, 109
Claudel, Paul, 118
Coleridge, S. T., 107
Colour, 10, 11, 20, 34, 41, 42, 70, 104, 111, 117
Common nature, 37, 65, 76, 114, 117
Condren, Father, 108
Consolation, 29, 63
Constable, John, 10
Cook, E. T., 103
Corpus Christi, 77
Correspondence, see Analogy
Counterpoint, 55, 76, 82-7, 115
Crashaw, Richard, 96
Creation, 25, 26, 27, 28, 33-9, 43, 44, 50, 51, 52, 53, 57, 58, 62, 64, 65, 67, 76, 80, 93, 94, 95, 100, 104, 111, 116
Curvature, 25, 26, 27, 59, 65, 79, 100, 104, 106-7, 109

Daniélou, Jean, 110
D'Arcy, Martin, S.J., 5
da Vinci, Leonardo, 111
de Digulleville, Guillaume, 109
de Mornay, Philippe, 106
Desolation, 29, 88-91, 99, 116
Devil, 58, 69, 76
Devlin, Christopher, S.J., 5, 103, 106, 108, 110, 112

123

Index

Index

Index

Index